Experiencing

Life and Power

through
Biblical
Meditation

Experiencing

Life and Power

through
Biblical
Meditation

May the words of my mouth
and the meditation of my heart
be pleasing in Your sight,
O LORD, my Rock and my Redeemer.
King David – Psalm 19:14

Dennis Fuqua

Experiencing
Life and Power
through
Biblical
Meditation
© 2015 Dennis Fuqua

Published by L/P Press
Vancouver, WA. USA
www.lppress.net

International Standard Book Number

ISBN-13: 978-1503250666
ISBN-10: 1503250660
BISAC: Religion / Christian Life / Personal Growth

Cover design and publishing assistance by Dan Mayhew (www.twoworldsmedia.com). Cover photo by Dennis Fuqua.

All Scripture quotations, unless otherwise indicated, are taken from the Holy Bible, New International Version, Copyright © 1973, 1978, 1984, 2011 by International Bible Society. Used by permission.

Scriptures identified as ESV are taken from The Holy Bible, English Standard Version. Copyright © 2001 by Crossway Bibles, a division of Good News Publishers. Used by permission.

Table of Contents

Are You Ready?   1

1. Our Need for Biblical Meditation   3

2. The Role of Biblical Meditation   11

3. The Value of Biblical Meditation   25

4. The Meaning of Biblical Meditation   41

5. Some Examples of Biblical Meditation   57

6. The Goal of Biblical Meditation   65

7. The Process of Biblical Meditation   71

8. The Objects of Biblical Meditation   81

9. A Demonstration of Biblical Meditation   89

10. Some Suggestions for Biblical Meditation   101

And Finally...   115

About the Books   119

About the Author   123

Now It's Your Turn...   125

Are You Ready?

It was a time when the church was booming. People were getting saved every day, dynamic miracles were taking place, great times of fellowship and teaching, and the culture was noticing. It was happening!

But it was during this time that the first church split could have easily taken place (Acts 6). If you have ever been through a church split, you know the pain it can cause. You know it is serious. In this case, one group was claiming they were not being treated equally with another group. The Apostles and other leaders were approached and asked to fix the problem.

The leaders listened, and agreed that there was a problem. But their response was very different than what we might expect. They opted to delegate this problem to others. "What? You call that good leadership?" In fact, the leaders said it would not be right for them to neglect what God had called them to do to address this problem. "Well, you can't do that!"

They did this not because they were unwilling to help, but because they were unwilling to stop giving themselves to a higher priority: *to prayer and the ministry of the Word.*[1]

These two priorities – prayer and the ministry of the Word – were the priorities of the early church leaders. I believe they should also be the priorities of every believer

---

[1] Acts 6:4

today: especially spiritual leaders. Prayer and the Word were the solutions back then. They are still the solutions today.

I have written two books are on the topic of prayer – personal and corporate. It seems this book naturally follows. There are many ways we should interact with Scripture. This book will show you how to be meaningfully engaged in the most important way to interact with Scripture.

No one would say meditating on Scripture is a bad thing. But there are too few of us who say it is an essential thing for spiritual growth!

- Do you know the stunning Scriptural promises for those who practice Biblical meditation?
- What does it mean to meditate? Do you know how to do it?
- What difference will it make in my life if I do this?
- What's the goal of Biblical meditation?
- What should I meditate about?
- How do I know when I am doing it right?

These are just a few of the questions this book will clearly address.

There is no guarantee that reading this book will change your life. But, if you read it and do what it says, there is a Biblical guarantee that your life will never be the same.

Are you ready? Let's start out by looking at our need for Biblical meditation. But first, let's pray. "God, open the eyes of my heart to see my need for meditating on Your Word."

Chapter 1

Meditation is simply talking to God about His Word with a desire that your life and those you pray for come into agreement with it.

~ William Thrasher

Our Need for Biblical Meditation

God is a God who communicates. He began speaking in Genesis 1 and He is still speaking in Revelation 22.

There is nothing else like God's communication: whether we call it His Word, His law, His statutes, His decrees, His precepts, etc. Whatever we call it, when God communicates, things are no longer the same. Moses told the people that God's words were their life.[2] Jesus told both His followers and detractors the same thing.[3] Hebrews 4:12 states that the Word of God is alive and powerful, or living and active.[4]

---

[2] Deuteronomy 32:47 They are not just idle words for you—they are your life. By them you will live long in the land you are crossing the Jordan to possess.

[3] John 6:63 …The words I have spoken to you—they are spirit and life.

[4] Hebrews 4:12 For the word of God is alive and active...

God's communication produces Life and Power. He spoke and worlds came into existence.[5] The Gospel of John tells us that *without Him* (the Living Word) *nothing was made that has been made.*[6] In fact, Psalm 33:6 indicates He just w-h-i-s-p-e-r-e-d (used His breath) and all the stars were made.[7] He raised Lazarus by speaking to him, even when he was dead.[8] That is power. That is life.

Since the time Adam and Eve sinned, all of us have needed that Life and Power. We need it to enter God's Family and we need it to live properly in His Family.

Look at what Paul writes to believers in Ephesians 4:17-18. *So I tell you this, and insist on it in the Lord, that you must no longer live as the Gentiles do, in the futility of their thinking.* [18] *They are darkened in their understanding and separated from the life of God because of the ignorance that is in them due to the hardening of their hearts.* Here are three key points.

- Those of us who know God must live no longer like those who don't know God.
- Those who do not know God live the way they do because of the way they think. Their understanding is darkened.
- This is because of the condition of their heart.

---

[5] Genesis 1:3 And God said, "Let there be light," and there was light. (See also v. 6, 9, 11, 14, etc.)

[6] John 1:3

[7] Psalm 33:6 By the word of the LORD the heavens were made, their starry host by the breath of his mouth.

[8] John 11:43 When he had said this, Jesus called in a loud voice, "Lazarus, come out!"

We need something strong enough to change both our minds and our hearts. God's Word, and the Life and Power it contains, is designed to do just that. That is why we need His Word. It is only as His Word (Written and Living) impacts us that we experience that Life and Power and a change in our minds and hearts.

How does it impact us most deeply? How can we cooperate with God to let it do its work in us? I am convinced the most impactful way Scripture affects us is through the process of meditation.

Meditation is how His Word produces His Life and Power in our lives. It is how the Spirit of God writes the Word of God on the hearts of the people of God.

He values communication so much that He calls His only and deeply loved Son *the Word*.[9] When God decided to come to earth, to demonstrate the nature of the Father,[10] He chose to be called *the Word of God*.[11] When God wanted to give us the story of His love and interaction with us, He did it through words.[12] So

> *Meditation is how the Spirit of God writes the Word of God on the hearts of the people of God.*

---

[9] John 1:1 In the beginning was the Word, and the Word was with God, and the Word was God.

[10] John 17:6 I have revealed you (your name) to those whom you gave me out of the world. (See also v. 26)

[11] John 1:14 The Word became flesh and made his dwelling among us.

[12] 2 Timothy 3:16 All Scripture is God-breathed and is useful for teaching, rebuking, correcting and training in righteousness...

we have a Living Word of God (Jesus Christ) and a Written Word of God (the Scriptures). Both provide Life and Power.

God's Word is not simply a book written by men. It is what it claims to be: God's eternal Word written as He has directed.[13] It did not become true because someone said it was true. It did not become true when it was written down or translated. It has always been true.[14] When it was put in written form, it was simply an accurate record of what had always been true. He describes this communication as being both inspired by Him (God breathed) and profitable (useful).[15]

Because the Word is God-breathed, it is true, trustworthy,[16] sure and reliable.[17]

Then, notice several statements the Bible makes about its usefulness. Here is a partial list of the many amazing ways His Word is useful in our lives. It is at work in those who

---

[13] 2 Peter 1:21 For prophecy never had its origin in the human will, but prophets, though human, spoke from God as they were carried along by the Holy Spirit.

[14] Psalm 119:89 Your word, LORD, is eternal; it stands firm in the heavens.

[15] 2 Timothy 3:16 (See above)

[16] Numbers 23:19 God is not human, that he should lie, not a human being, that he should change his mind. Does he speak and then not act? Does he promise and not fulfill? (See also John 8:30-32; 17:17; Titus 1:2)

[17] Psalm 119:86 All your commands are trustworthy; help me, for I am being persecuted without cause. (See also Matthew 5;17-18; John 10:35; I Peter 1:25)

believe.[18] It makes us wise to salvation,[19] nourishes us,[20] strengthens us,[21] sanctifies us[22] and equips us for service.[23] It builds us up and gives us an inheritance among the saints.[24] The Word fills us with light,[25] gives direction for our lives,[26] and gives us endurance, comfort, and encouragement.[27] It revives us and makes us wise,[28] delivers us

---

[18] 1 Thessalonians 2:13 And we also thank God continually because, when you received the word of God, which you heard from us, you accepted it not as a human word, but as it actually is, the word of God, which is indeed at work in you who believe.

[19] 2 Timothy 3:15 and how from infancy you have known the Holy Scriptures, which are able to make you wise for salvation through faith in Christ Jesus.

[20] Matthew 4:4 Jesus answered, "It is written: 'Man shall not live on bread alone, but on every word that comes from the mouth of God.'" (See also I Peter 2:2)

[21] Psalm 119:28 My soul is weary with sorrow; strengthen me according to your word.

[22] John 17:17 Sanctify them by the truth; your word is truth.

[23] 2 Timothy 3:17 so that the servant of God may be thoroughly equipped for every good work.

[24] Acts 20:32 Now I commit you to God and to the word of his grace, which can build you up and give you an inheritance among all those who are sanctified.

[25] Psalm 119:130 The unfolding of your words gives light; it gives understanding to the simple.

[26] Proverbs 3:6 in all your ways submit to him, and he will make your paths straight.

[27] Romans 15:4 For everything that was written in the past was written to teach us, so that through the endurance taught in the Scriptures and the encouragement they provide we might have hope.

[28] Psalm 19:7 The law of the LORD is perfect, refreshing the soul. The statutes of the LORD are trustworthy, making wise the simple.

and preserves us from sin,[29] heals us,[30] cleanses us and
makes us godly[31] and gives us faith.[32]

These things (and many others) give us plenty of reason
to give great value to His Word. David did. He valued it so
much that the longest Psalm – which is also the longest
chapter and prayer in the Bible – Psalm 119, is dedicated to
declaring and describing its value.[33] All but 5 of the 176
verses refer to God's Communication to us in some manner.
As you read this Psalm you get some sense of his fanatical
love for what God says.

My hope is that as you move through these pages you
will value God's Word more and more. But my hope goes
beyond that. I deeply desire that as you spend time meditating upon it for years to come, you will also experience more
of His Life and His Power. I want the seed of God's
Word[34] to not only be planted in your heart, but to grow and
produce an abundant harvest. That is what we need and
that is what meditation does.

---

[29] Psalm 119:9 How can a young person stay on the path of purity?
By living according to your word.

[30] Psalm 107:20 He sent out his word and healed them; he res-
cued them from the grave.

[31] Ephesians 5:26 to make her holy, cleansing[a] her by the washing with water through the word,

[32] Romans 10:17 Consequently, faith comes from hearing the message, and the message is heard through the word about Christ.

[33] This reflects the traditional view that David wrote this Psalm.
Though it is possible someone else wrote it, we know of David's high
view of God's Word and meditation from Psalm 19 and other places.

[34] Luke 8:11 This is the meaning of the parable: The seed is the
word of God.

Throughout this book I want to introduce you to some of my friends and their experiences with Biblical meditation. Here is Scott…

I have served the Lord for well over 30 years. In my late teens and early twenties I immersed myself in meditating and memorizing Scripture. The Word of God was my foundation, my center point. Over three decades of being a husband, a father, a pastor and businessman, it is what I have held onto through the good, the bad, and the difficult.

Now, in my fifties, I have never been more aware of my desperate need to continue to anchor all of my life on Scripture. I have successfully navigated 30 years of marriage, raising four highly successful children, pastored a vibrant and growing church that I passed onto a spiritual son and achieved a level of accomplishment in the business world that many would dream to experience. And… I have never been more desperate, committed, driven to meditate, memorize and ponder on God's Word. Not long ago the Lord said to me, "If meditating on My Word was the key to your success for the first 34 years of your adult life, then is it not the key to the next 34 years of your life?"

I can achieve all of the "right things" in life and undo all of it in one moment living outside of God's Word. The Word of God is not just my life line, it is my life. Reading Scripture informs me so that I might know the will of God. Meditating on Scripture transforms me so that I might live the will of God.

Reading Scripture informs me so I might know the will of God. Meditating on Scripture transforms me so I might live the will of God.

Now, let's consider the role Biblical meditation should play in our interaction with Scripture. But first, let's pray. "Thank You, Father, that you show us our need for Your Word. Now, let me see the role you want meditation to have in getting Your Word into my life."

Chapter 2

Read the Bible carefully, and then meditate and meditate and meditate... the more you meditate on it, the more you will be astonished with it.
~ C H Spurgeon

The Role of Biblical Meditation

What is the most impactful way we can interact with Scripture? There are several different ways, but what do you think is the best way? Well, since this is a book about Biblical meditation, that answer would probably be a pretty safe bet!

But before we consider the specifics of meditation, let's look briefly at two related topics: 1) why we should interact with Scripture at all, and 2) what are the other ways we can interact with Scripture. Each of these can be illustrated with our hands.

On One Hand

There are at least five specific reasons followers of Jesus should interact with the Word of God.

In order to know its content – Knowing what God's Word says is not the primary reason we should spend time in it, though it is important to know what God's Word says.

God charged each Old Testament king to hand-write his own personal copy of the Law.[35] This was God's way of making sure the king knew what was stated there. Paul instructed his young friend, Timothy, to be diligent to know the Scriptures and to handle them accurately.[36] Peter displayed great knowledge of Scripture when he spontaneously quoted at length from the book of Joel and two different Psalms on the day of Pentecost.[37] It is obvious that other New Testament writers were very familiar with the Old Testament as they wrote.[38]

Also, Jesus demonstrated on many occasions that He had a thorough knowledge of Scripture. It was the primary weapon He used against the evil one.[39] Knowing the content of Scripture in and of itself is not sufficient, but knowing it is the starting point to other significant uses of Scripture.

In order to have our minds renewed – In Romans 12:2, Paul summarized a key to spiritual growth. *Do not conform any longer to the pattern of this world, but be transformed by the renewing of your mind…*

---

[35] Deuteronomy 17:18 When he takes the throne of his kingdom, he is to write for himself on a scroll a copy of this law, taken from that of the Levitical priests.

[36] 2 Timothy 2:15 Do your best to present yourself to God as one approved, a worker who does not need to be ashamed and who correctly handles the word of truth.

[37] See Acts 2:17-21, 25-28, and 34-35

[38] Consider Paul in Romans and John in Revelation.

[39] Matthew 4:4 Jesus answered, "It is written: 'Man shall not live on bread alone, but on every word that comes from the mouth of God.'" (See also vv. 7 & 10)

Our thoughts are not naturally God's thoughts. His thoughts are higher than ours.[40] *But we have the mind of Christ.*[41] So we are to *Let the word of Christ dwell in (us) richly...*[42] so that our thoughts become more in line with His. As we spend time interacting with God's Word, the way we think (the way we view God, ourselves, other people, situations, and the world around us) can be transformed (the actual word in Romans 12:2 is the word from which we get our word *metamorphosis*). Our minds can not only be renewed, but they can also be cleansed as God's Word washes us.[43] This washing removes the residue left by living in this broken world. It makes our heart a cleaner slate on which God can write His message.

The direction we set our minds upon matters. In Romans 8, Paul goes so far as to say that *the mind set on the flesh is death, but the mind set on the Spirit is life and peace.*[44] A similar thought is mentioned by Isaiah. *You will keep him in perfect peace whose mind is stayed on You, because he trusts in You.*[45] Our minds have

> *As we spend time interacting with God's Word, the way we think can be transformed.*

---

[40] Isaiah 55:9 As the heavens are higher than the earth, so are my ways higher than your ways and my thoughts than your thoughts.

[41] 1 Corinthians 2:16b

[42] Colossians 3:16

[43] Ephesians 5:26 to make her holy, cleansing her by the washing with water through the word,

[44] Romans 8:6

[45] Isaiah 26:3

been designed to function best when they are at peace. Setting our mind to be open to and subject to what God says restores it because it puts it at peace.

In order to have our souls renewed – I served as a pastor in a congregation for many years. During this time I concluded that nearly all relational problems people spoke with me about were the direct result of their souls not experiencing rest. By *soul* I am referring to what could be called our *psyche*. No need to be afraid of this word. It is Biblical. It is the Greek word that refers to that inner part of us, which processes and directs our emotions, attitudes, thoughts and decisions. It includes our mind (see above) but it is more than just our mind.

Jesus addresses this in Matthew 11:28-30. *Come to me, all you who are weary and burdened, and I will give you rest. Take my yoke upon you and learn from me, for I am gentle and humble in heart, and you will find rest for your souls.[46] For my burden is easy and my burden is light.*

Our souls were designed by God to live in peace. Living in this broken world gives our souls many opportunities to lose that peace. When that happens our soul needs its rest restored.

As we learn gentleness and humility from Jesus, our souls will experience the rest and peace they were designed for. This allows us to interact with people and situations – even difficult ones – in a way Jesus would. Letting His

---

[46] This is the Greek word *psyche*

Spirit live out the beatitudes[47] and the fruit of the Spirit[48] through our lives are also ways our souls are renewed.

It is helpful to see salvation as a process in which our spirits are already saved, our bodies will one day be saved, and our souls are in the process of being saved right now. We have been saved from the penalty of sin. One day, we will be saved from the very presence of sin. But right now, we can be saved from the power of sin. This is the salvation we are experiencing right now. Our souls are being saved. This is what it means to be (becoming) *conformed to the image of Jesus*,[49] or to have *Christ... formed in (us)*,[50] or to *work out our salvation with fear and trembling*.[51] Present interaction with God's Word saves (restores) our soul.[52]

In order to obey God – Knowing the content of Scripture and having our minds and our souls repaired, are essential steps in our maturity, but the reason we are to know the content of Scripture and the reason we are to be conformed to His image is for us to do what God says.

Obeying God (not out of a heart of legalism, but out of a heart of love and gratitude) has always been a major reason God tells us His standards. This is the reason He spoke the

---

[47] Matthew 5:3-10

[48] Galatians 5:22-23

[49] Romans 8:29

[50] Galatians 4:19

[51] Philippians 2:12

[52] James 1:21 (ESV) Therefore put away all filthiness and rampant wickedness and receive with meekness the implanted word, which is able to save your souls. (See also Ps 19:7)

Ten Commandments. He wants people to obey Him *so that it may go well with them and their children forever!*[53] A key reason God told Joshua to meditate on His Word was *so that you may be careful to do everything written in it. Then you will be prosperous and successful.*[54] And Jesus said specifically, *If you love me, you will obey what I command.*[55] Time invested in interacting with God's Word will result in His promise fulfilled in us. It will go well with us because we have obeyed.

In order to know God – The four reasons mentioned above are wonderful and worthy of serious consideration, but they are not the primary reason interaction with God's Word is so valuable to His followers. In His longest and most intense prayer, Jesus describes eternal life as knowing *You, the only true God and Jesus Christ, whom You have sent.*[56] Jesus defines the quality of our life – temporal and eternal – as the level to which we *know* the Source of Life. We are not to boast in our wisdom, our abilities, or our accumulations. But we are to boast that we know the character of God.[57]

---

[53] Deuteronomy 5:29

[54] Joshua 1:8

[55] John 14:15

[56] John 17:3

[57] Jeremiah 9:23-24 (ESV) Thus says the LORD: "Let not the wise man boast in his wisdom, let not the mighty man boast in his might, let not the rich man boast in his riches, [24] but let him who boasts boast in this, that he understands and knows me, that I am the LORD who practices steadfast love, justice, and righteousness in the earth. For in these things I delight, declares the LORD."

In the most emotional chapter Paul wrote, he contrasted his legalistic way of life with the overflowing joy of knowing Jesus.[58] He counted everything else

Jesus defines the quality of our life – temporal and eternal – as the level to which we know the Source of Life.

as worthless! Knowing God (Father, Son, and Holy Spirit) is what makes sense out of life. It is what gives value, meaning, and direction to life. Knowing Him. Relating to Him. Reveling in Him. Receiving His love. Enjoying Him. Walking with Him. Being with Him.

When the Apostle John considered the "hell on earth" he and the world would go through before he would be with Jesus again, he exclaimed, *Amen. Come Lord Jesus.*[59]

Since all relationships are determined and defined by the level of communication in those relationships, our relationship with the Triune God will be defined by the way we interact with His Word.

These five reasons can be illustrated by looking at our hand. Knowing its content is like our "pinky" finger. It is there, but needs help. To have our minds renewed is like "ring man." We are regularly renewing our covenant relationship with Jesus. Having our souls find rest and renewal is like "tall man." Our souls are coming into agreement and alignment with the Savior. "Pointer" reminds us of obedi-

---

[58] Philippians 3:7 But whatever were gains to me I now consider loss for the sake of Christ. (See Phil 3:4b-11)
[59] Revelation 22:20

ence. It points us in the proper direction. And "thumbkin" which is the strongest and stands out the most, represents knowing God.

And On the Other Hand

The Navigators have, for many years, used an illustration of a hand to list the five ways we interact with Scripture. It is still a very helpful tool. Each way has unique value.

Our "pinky" represents **hearing** *God's Word* – The great cry of the Israelites which comes from Deuteronomy 6:4 was to *"Hear, Oh Israel..."* In fact, God calls His people to *hear* (or harken to) what He says at least 55 times in the book of Deuteronomy alone. It should be noted that this hearing assumes not simply hearing, but receiving and obeying. The reason for our hearing is that we would respond and receive Life from God. In Romans 10:17 Paul states that *faith comes by hearing...* Paul told Timothy to give reading Scripture its proper place.[60] It is evident that Paul wanted the Scriptures read so people would hear them. It is through hearing that the initial message of Jesus and the ongoing messages of Jesus comes to us.

Our "ring man" represents **reading** *God's Word* – This is a staple for receiving nourishment from the Lord. It is clear that each of the writers of Scripture were also readers of it. They reference other Scriptures regularly. They knew

---

[60] 1 Timothy 4:13 Until I come, devote yourself to the public reading of Scripture, to preaching and to teaching.

the Scriptures because they read them often. One of the primary reasons the Jewish synagogue existed was to teach their children how to read the Scriptures. In American history a primary reason schools developed in the 18th and 19th centuries was to teach children how to read so they could read the Scriptures. Regularly reading larger sections of Scripture is a primary means of getting the truth of God into our minds and hearts.

Our "tall man" represents **studying** *God's Word –* Studying goes beyond reading and helps us both synthesize (noting how truths can be "put together") and analyze (noting how truths can be "taken apart") Scripture. It takes time and effort to develop good study habits. Many books and courses are available to help develop these habits. It is worth it to give ourselves to learn and practice good, accurate Bible study methods. The best courses do not simply tell you what to believe, but how to dive into God's Word so you can find the answers yourself. I saw my Bible School training as a multiple-year entry course on how to study the Bible for the rest of my life.

Our "pointer" represents **memorizing** *God's Word –* As we hear, read, and study Scripture, we come across verses that speak specifically to us or a situation we may be facing. Committing that verse to memory allows us to keep thinking about it throughout our day and for years to come. David refers to hiding *God's word in his heart.*[61] He said it over and over until he knew it word for word. This allowed

---

[61] Psalm 119:11

19

him to take it with him when his scrolls were not available. He always had it *in his heart.*

When memorized, God's Word can become not only a comfort to us, but also a weapon for us. Consider how Jesus used verses He had memorized when He faced the temptation from the evil one.[62] It is how He resisted the devil and how we can too.[63]

Finally, *our "thumbkin" represents* **meditating** *on God's Word.* Since this is the topic of this book, much more on this will follow. At this point I simply want to emphasize two things about this illustration.

First, each of the first four ways we interact with Scripture are not complete until we meditate. We do not get the value out of hearing, reading, studying, or memorizing until we truly meditate upon what God is saying.

Remember the illustration of the hand. Now take a moment and touch each of your fingers with your thumb. Just as our thumb can easily interact with each of our fingers, so also meditation should be the end result of hearing, reading, studying, and memorizing Scripture.

> *We do not get the value out of hearing, reading, studying, or memorizing until we truly meditate upon what God is saying.*

Second, we may be able to pick up an object using only our fingers, but it is awkward. But we cannot *grasp* an ob-

---

[62] Matthew 4;4, 7, & 10
[63] James 4:7 Submit yourselves, then, to God. Resist the devil, and he will flee from you.

ject using only our fingers. We can only grasp an object by using our thumb. In a similar manner, we cannot really *grasp* Scripture until we meditate upon it.

Here is a story from my friend, Jeremy...

In the 20 years I have been following Christ the most significant and most shaping moments for me have been when the truth of God's Word became "radioactive." What I mean by "radioactive" is when, in a moment, a certain truth about God goes from being intellectually understood and confined to my brain to penetrating every aspect of my being. Suddenly what I thought to be true about God is no longer sufficient compared to what I now see. It is as if the entire world is now colored in a different light as a result of this truth. It has come alive to me in living color and I know that I will never be the same again. Almost exclusively, these moments have come about as a result of meditation. What follows is a brief account of one of my more dramatic moments of meditation.

One week in the fall of 2012 I was preparing for a sermon in which I was going to be referencing Isaiah 61:1-3. It was not my main text but was going to be referred to in my conclusion. I have always loved this passage. So I thought I would take some extra time to meditate on it a bit.

First I read it several times almost to the point where I could quote it from memory. Then I studied it a bit and looked at some of the Hebrew words used in it. Next I "chewed" on it for a bit... mulling it over in my mind and basking in the beauty of the passage. Finally, a little later in the day when I was having some private prayer time, I asked the Lord to "marinate" my heart with his desires.

Then I remembered Isaiah 61:1-3 again. I felt led to begin praying from it. Line by line I began to go through the passage and let my prayers be shaped by the truths in it. When I was praying from the part that says, He has sent me... to proclaim freedom for the captives, something happened: this passage became "radioactive."

At once, I became completely overwhelmed by the mercy and grace of Christ. I knew that Jesus had come to proclaim freedom to the captives, but suddenly, now I knew it. I fell to the ground and began to weep as I tried to continue to pray. Every time I tried to pray I would again be overcome and fall to the ground weeping. This continued for about the next 40 minutes as the Lord marinated my heart with His desires. I began to understand the love of Christ and the purpose of the Church in a brand new way. That moment forever changed the way I saw the world and my place in it as a follower of Christ.

On one hand, we interact with Scripture *in order to…*

- know its content
- have our minds restored
- have our souls restored
- obey it,
- and to know God.

On the other hand, we interact with Scripture *by*...

- hearing it
- reading it
- studying it
- memorizing it
- and meditating upon it.

What's the role of Biblical meditation? It is the best and most effective way followers of Jesus can interact with God's Word. Nothing accomplishes the purpose of His Word in our life like meditation.

Now let's consider the value of meditation. What does it do for us? How are we different because we meditate? But first, let's pray. "Father, thank You for the incredible power of Your Word. Open the eyes of my heart to see the value of developing a life-style of meditating upon it."

Chapter 3

Scripture is wonderful, if you meditate on it. Our problem is we read without meditation. Your life will never be anchored like a tree without meditation.
~ Henry Blackaby

The Value of Biblical Meditation

Before we look at some specific definitions and illustrations of what meditation is and what it looks like later in this book, let's look at its value. Why should we take time to learn this skill? What difference can it make in my life?

Scripture is very specific and clear about what can happen if and when people meditate on what God says. We will look at three key Scriptures. Let's start with Joshua 1:8.[64]

Joshua 1:8

Joshua's story does not begin in Joshua chapter 1. He was one of only two Egypt-born Israelites to make it all the

---

[64] Joshua 1:8 Keep this Book of the Law always on your lips; meditate on it day and night, so that you may be careful to do everything written in it. Then you will be prosperous and successful.

way into the Promised Land.[65]   Along the way, he served Moses well, though he did not always have the best discernment.[66]

He first appears in Scripture as the young man Moses called to fight the Amalekites soon after they crossed the Red Sea.   As Moses prayed, Joshua fought, and won.[67] Joshua became Moses' aid and was with him on Mount Sinai when Moses received the original Ten Commandments.[68]   In fact, it was Joshua who first heard the noise coming from the Israelite camp indicating something was not right.[69]   Later on, as Moses and God were processing what the next chapter should be for the Israelites, Joshua stayed at the tent of meeting after Moses had left.[70]   He evidently loved being in the presence of God.

---

[65] Numbers 14:30 Not one of you will enter the land I swore with uplifted hand to make your home, except Caleb son of Jephunneh and Joshua son of Nun.

[66] Numbers 11:28 Joshua son of Nun, who had been Moses' aide since youth, spoke up and said, "Moses, my lord, stop them!"

[67] Exodus 17:11 As long as Moses held up his hands, the Israelites were winning, but whenever he lowered his hands, the Amalekites were winning. (See Ex 17:8-13)

[68] Exodus 24:13 Then Moses set out with Joshua his aide, and Moses went up on the mountain of God. (See also Numbers 11:28)

[69] Exodus 32:17 When Joshua heard the noise of the people shouting, he said to Moses, "There is the sound of war in the camp."

[70] Exodus 33:11 The LORD would speak to Moses face to face, as one speaks to a friend. Then Moses would return to the camp, but his young aide Joshua son of Nun did not leave the tent.

He was selected as the one to represent the tribe of Ephraim to explore the land of Canaan.[71] After the twelve spies checked out the land, and the ten spies gave the report that they should have never left Egypt, it was only Joshua and Caleb who grieved at their lack of confidence in God.[72]

God told Moses, and Moses told the people, that Joshua would be the one to lead them into the Promised Land. But he needed encouragement on several occasions.[73] And prior to Moses' death, God both commissioned Joshua to be the leader of the Nation,[74] and also filled him with a spirit of wisdom.[75] This caused the people of Israel to listen to and obey him.

This is where the story picks up in Joshua chapter 1. Joshua was already an experienced warrior and a called leader when God gave him the significant task of replacing Moses. He was to lead the next generation of Israelites into

---

[71] Numbers 13:8&16 **8** from the tribe of Ephraim, Hoshea son of Nun;**16** These are the names of the men Moses sent to explore the land. (Moses gave Hoshea son of Nun the name Joshua.)

[72] Numbers 14:6 Joshua son of Nun and Caleb son of Jephunneh, who were among those who had explored the land, tore their clothes (See Numbers 14:1-9)

[73] Deuteronomy 1:38 But your assistant, Joshua son of Nun, will enter it. Encourage him, because he will lead Israel to inherit it. (See also 3:21, 28, 31:7-8, 23)

[74] Deuteronomy 31:14 The LORD said to Moses, "Now the day of your death is near. Call Joshua and present yourselves at the tent of meeting, where I will commission him." So Moses and Joshua came and presented themselves at the tent of meeting.

[75] Deuteronomy 34:9 Now Joshua son of Nun was filled with the spirit[a] of wisdom because Moses had laid his hands on him. So the Israelites listened to him and did what the LORD had commanded Moses.

the land God had in mind for them since they left Egypt. He needed to be successful. Not just for his sake, but for the sake of the Nation depending upon him. And most of all, for the sake of the Name of His God. If he was going to be successful, he needed strength and courage. This was what Moses and God had told him *prior to* this chapter and also three times *in* this chapter.[76]

Into this setting, we have the command for Joshua to meditate on what God had said.

Near the end of this 8-verse challenge, in Joshua 1:8, God says... *Do not let this Book of the Law depart from your mouth; meditate on it day and night, so that you may be careful to do everything written in it. You will be prosperous and successful.*

This Book of the Law refers specifically to the books of Moses, the first five books of the Old Testament. But in the larger sense, it refers to all the things God had spoken. What He had spoken in general and what He had spoken specifically to Joshua. This is what Joshua was to meditate upon.

For Joshua, meditation looked like keeping what God said always *in his mouth*. It was not to depart from him – not in the sense that it was not to be spoken, but in the sense that it was always to be right there available for him. This is reiterated with the words, *day and night*. Whatever else meditation is, it was to be an all-the-time thing for Joshua.

---

[76] Joshua 1:6 Be strong and courageous, because you will lead these people to inherit the land I swore to their ancestors to give them. (See also v. 7 & 9)

The words *so that* point us to the reason God called Joshua to meditate. Meditation brings us to a place where we are *careful to do everything* God says. Meditation leads to obedience. There is something about meditation that allows God's truth to trickle from our heads to our hearts and through our hearts to our lives. This is what Joshua needed. It is what we need as well.

This, then, leads to *prosperity and success*. The word *prosperity* means to make progress or advance. We were not made to stand still. We were made to move forward. Prosperity does not speak so much about where we are as much as it does about where we are going. Being successful in the journey.

> *There is something about meditation that allows God's truth to trickle from our heads to our hearts and through our hearts to our lives.*

Joshua could not stand still and accomplish God's mission for him. Neither can we. Meditation moves us forward from where we are to where we need to be.

Over half the times the word for *success* is used, it is translated with words like *understanding* and *wisdom*. We do not naturally have this kind of successful perspective. We need to acquire if from an outside source. Joshua needed wisdom and understanding beyond himself to accomplish God's mission. So do we. Meditation gives us success in our calling because it helps us gain God's understanding and wisdom.

For Joshua, prosperity and success looked like *strength* and *courage*. Now, look what happened after he began meditating on God's Word. After multiple commands to Joshua from Moses to be strong and courageous *prior to* Joshua 1 and in this exchange with God *in* Joshua 1, this challenge was no longer spoken to Joshua. He became the one telling others to *be strong and courageous!*[77] He needed strength and courage. Through meditation, he got it! Now he is the one who is challenging and encouraging others to receive it.

What does success look like for you? What do you need from God? Do you need humility? Vision? Direction? Confidence? Compassion? The Word of God contains those things for you. They will become yours as it is written on your heart through meditation.

Prosperity and success are key results of meditation. These two things come about through obedience to what God says. And obedience comes from continual meditation.

Here is a brief way of viewing Joshua 1:8.

Continuous meditation leads to *obedience* which leads to *wise understanding* and *advancement*, which (in Joshua's case) led to *strength* and *courage*.

I want to stand in that line.

---

[77] Joshua 10:25 Joshua said to them, "Do not be afraid; do not be discouraged. Be strong and courageous. This is what the LORD will do to all the enemies you are going to fight."

Psalm 1:1-3

A second key Scripture about the value of Biblical meditation is Psalm 1:1-3

¹Blessed is the man who does not walk in the counsel of the wicked or stand in the way of sinners or sit in the seat of mockers. ²But his delight is in the law of the LORD, and on his law he meditates day and night. ³He is like a tree planted by streams of water, which yields its fruit in season and whose leaf does not wither. Whatever he does prospers.

When David wrote this Psalm,[78] he did not know it would be the first of 150 Psalms. But it is so appropriate that the Book of Psalms begins with these words! In a very real sense, all the other Psalms flow from this one. The Psalms are a collection of personal experiences run through the grid of God's Word. They are written by people who were saturated in what God said because they had meditated upon it. It became their point of reference for understanding their circumstances, their life, and therefore their writing.

In one sense, all of the Psalms are the result of meditation upon what God has said, mixed with a variety of human situations and emotions. To launch us into all the rest of the Psalms, we have these words about the value of meditation.

---

[78] This reflects the traditional view that David wrote this Psalm. Though it is possible someone else wrote it, we know of David's high view of God's Word and meditation from Psalm 19 and other places.

Verse one states the value of not receiving bad input. Our lives are better off when we reject input from those who do not like or follow God's Word or ways. We live better when we seek to influence these people rather than be influenced by them.

We see the contrast of this in verse two. Our lives will be blessed when we do receive the input from God's communication to us. Again the phrase *law of the LORD* does not have to be limited to either the Ten Commandments or the first five books of the Bible. It can be seen here as all that God communicates to us.

David *delighted* in what God said. In fact, it was because he delighted in it that he meditated upon it. To the degree we delight in it, to that same degree we will meditate upon it. He was familiar enough with Scripture to know that when God spoke, it was good to obey it. This may seem so obvious, but consider a key event in David's life.

When David became king, the Ark of the Covenant – which represented the very presence of God – was not in the Holy of Holies. It was in the possession of God's enemies, the Philistines. David wanted to take care of this. The first attempt did not go so well for anybody, especially Uzzah.[79] The whole story can be read in 1 Chronicles 13 and 15.

> To the degree we delight in it, to that same degree we will meditate upon it.

---

[79] 1 Chronicles 13:9-10 When they came to the threshing floor of Kidon, Uzzah reached out his hand to steady the ark, because the oxen

Later, after a few more battle victories, David came to understand that the reason Uzzah experienced the Lord's anger was because he (David) had not *inquired of the LORD* just how the Ark was to be moved.[80] David's normal pattern was to seek the Lord about battles,[81] but, for some reason, it did not occur to him he should do the same in how to move the Ark. This event helped bring David to a point of delighting in what God says. When we obey Him, life goes well. When we don't obey Him, it can produce death.

There are four specific benefits to meditating on God's law listed in verse 3.

He is like a tree planted by streams of water – A tree planted by streams of water has two clear advantages. First, its root system is strong enough to hold it up even during significant times of storm. Second, its root system can cause it to receive nourishment because it is close to the source of water. As we meditate, our root system develops so we are able to be strong in the storm and receive nourishment when others, who are far from the source, may not.

---

stumbled. [10] The LORD's anger burned against Uzzah, and he struck him down because he had put his hand on the ark. So he died there before God.

[80] 1 Chronicles 15:13 It was because you, the Levites, did not bring it up the first time that the LORD our God broke out in anger against us. We did not inquire of him about how to do it in the prescribed way.

[81] 1 Chronicles 14:13-14 Once more the Philistines raided the valley; [14] so David inquired of God again, and God answered him, "Do not go directly after them, but circle around them and attack them in front of the poplar trees."

It yields its fruit in season – That is, because of its good root system, there is never a season when it is barren. The purpose of fruit, whether in the physical or the spiritual realm, is never for the tree. It is always for someone else. The nine fruit of the Spirit mentioned in Galatians 5[82] are the Spirit's fruit He wants to get to other people through us.

So, when other people "pick" on us (pun intended), that is simply an opportunity for us to be a blessing to them. Sometimes they deserve it, sometimes they don't. Either way, as we meditate upon God's Word, we will be fruitful in all seasons.

Whose leaf does not wither – One of the great needs of our day is followers of Jesus Christ who do *not* need to be revived. The reason people need to be re-vived is because they are not walking in the "vive" (life) that is continually available in Jesus. A command to the Old Testament priests was to make sure that the fire on the altar never went out.[83] This is a need for us today.

As New Testament priests, one of our first responsibilities each day is to check the condition of the fire on the altar of our heart. If it needs attention we are to add some wood (truth from God's Word about who He is and what

---

[82] See Galatians 5:22-23 But the fruit of the Spirit is love, joy, peace, forbearance, kindness, goodness, faithfulness, [23] gentleness and self-control. Against such things there is no law.

[83] Leviticus 6:12-13 The fire on the altar must be kept burning; it must not go out. Every morning the priest is to add firewood and arrange the burnt offering on the fire and burn the fat of the fellowship offerings on it. [13] The fire must be kept burning on the altar continuously; it must not go out.

He desires) and arrange it so that the fire in our hearts burns well throughout the day. This fire allows us to enjoy deeper and deeper fellowship with Him. What would it be like if every believer you know lived each day with this fire of love for God and His ways burning in their heart?

It is good to receive good teaching and preaching from others. But if we are depending upon that for all our spiritual nourishment, it will not be sufficient. Those who meditate on God's law experience continual renewal. Their leaf does not wither and die off. They always demonstrate the life of Jesus in them to others.

The final benefit for the meditator is that *whatever he does prospers* – This is the same word used in Joshua 1:8. Advancement. Progress. Forward movement. Increase. Successful journey.

> *As New Testament priests, one of our first responsibilities each day is to check the condition of the fire on the altar of our heart.*

This verse adds to that by using the word *whatever*. What a great word! It is a very broad word that is used over 2600 times in the Old Testament. It is all-inclusive. This *whatever* includes your spiritual life, your physical life, your relationships, your occupation, your finances, your past, your present, your future. Whatever. This Biblical promise is that those who meditate upon God's Word because they delight in it will see good progress in all areas of their lives.

Psalm 119:97-99

The final passage we will look at which communicates benefits of meditation is Psalm 119:97-99.

⁹⁷Oh, how I love Your law! I meditate on it all day long. ⁹⁸Your commands make me wiser than my enemies, for they are ever with me. ⁹⁹I have more insight than all my teachers, for I meditate on Your statutes.

As mentioned earlier, this Psalm is all about radical love for God's Word. So, it is not surprising to find the Psalmist link his love for it to meditating upon it.

Oh! How I love your law! – Do you catch the intensity of this cry? Meditating upon God's law is an expression not only of a love for it, but of a love for God. When we love someone, we love hearing from them. It is because I love my wife that I love talking with her. I love the sound of her voice and I love the content of what she says. Our love for God is reflected in how much we love what He says. Do you love Him? Do you love His Word? The natural outcome will be to meditate upon it – to savor it as long as we can.

Also notice again that meditation is an *all-day-long* thing for David. It is the same idea as we saw in both Joshua 1 and Psalm 1. Meditation can and should fit into everything else we are doing.

Wiser than my enemies – The wisdom that came to David was able to help him out-smart his enemies because it came from God Himself. When we meditate upon what God says, we will also gain wisdom to out-smart not only

36

the enemies around us, but primarily the enemy of our souls. Few things bring greater spiritual victory over the evil one like Biblical meditation. When we meditate, we begin to see the situation and the solution from God's perspective. This, then, allows us to fight with weapons beyond our own[84] and, as James 4:7 says, *Submit yourselves, then, to God, resist the devil, and he will flee from you.* There are few sights more pleasant than the back-side of the evil one leaving in a hurry.

I have more insight than all my teachers – This is not the battle motif, where someone is trying to harm you. It is a picture of the classroom, where someone is trying to help you. A teacher tries to help the student learn and grow. David knew that if he pondered what God said, he would not need to depend solely upon what others taught him. He could take what they said and go beyond where they went. Meditation on God's Word – letting it seep deep into your heart and life – will do that for you. You will be able to take the good instructions of others and build a stronger foundation because you have received things directly from the Lord.

> *When we meditate, we begin to see the situation and the solution from God's perspective.*

---

[84] See Romans 13:12 The night is nearly over; the day is almost here. So let us put aside the deeds of darkness and put on the armor of light. (See also 2 Corinthians 6:7, 10:4, Ephesians 6:10-17)

Consider this: the most profound truths you have ever heard from others are simply the result of their meditation upon the Scriptures. And the most meaningful lines of a song came from the meditation of the author. Continue to receive from others, but don't depend upon them for all your meals. Meditate on what God says so you can receive insight beyond what your best human teachers will ever say.

Here is a story from my friend, Phil...

I often find myself meditating without having it on my schedule. Like a recent experience at a ministry conference while listening to a sermon. The preacher was exceptional, so I was not easily distracted and certainly not disinterested. As he led us on our journey through Peter's rooftop prayer experience in Acts 11, I became stuck in verse 14 where Peter answers the Lord by saying "No!"

I've read and studied and heard this text before, but this time I was drawn deeply into the text and could not get out. The Holy Spirit had an insight for me that he would also turn into a message. That burst of reflection (I caught up again with the preacher after a few minutes) led to other moments of meditating on Scriptures revealing other times Peter had responded in a way he thought was obedience but probably wasn't.

Those times meditating, brief but fruitful, produced more than a sermon for preaching. The text became a mirror of responses based in my own sensibilities rather than in a clear understanding of the mind of Christ. Sometimes meditation is a combination of reflective moments that take us deeper and point us forward.

What is the value of Biblical meditation?

- It leads to obedience which leads to prosperity and success.
- It builds a solid root system for our lives.
- It allows us to produce continual fruit.
- It allows us to walk in continual renewal.
- It makes us wiser than our enemies.
- It teaches us better than our teachers.

Now that we have an understanding of the value of meditation, let's look at what it means to meditate. But first, let's pray. "Father, thank You for the value of Your Word. Would you now teach me what meditation is? Beyond the words of this book I ask that Your Spirit would speak and I would hear."

Chapter 4

The word meditate as used in the Old Testament literally means to murmur or to mutter and, by implication, to talk to oneself. When we meditate on the Scriptures we talk to ourselves about them, turning over in our minds the meanings, the implications, and the applications to our own lives.

~ Jerry Bridges

The Meaning of Biblical Meditation

So, what does Scripture mean when it refers to meditation? What was Joshua commanded to do? What was David doing? And what are we supposed to do? Is it different than the current trendy topic? If so, how?

The idea of meditation has been a universal human activity for many centuries. But it got a fresh boost in the late 60's when the Beatles made a trip to India and met a guru. I am not an expert on Eastern meditation, but my limited understanding is that its goal is to empty the mind of all thoughts and focus on as little as possible. A friend of mine who was saved out of the hippie movement jokingly described his experience with Eastern meditation as an invitation to "become one with nothing."

41

Though there are some similarities between this and Biblical meditation – such as slowing down and being intentional – I suggest that Biblical meditation is very different from either Eastern meditation or Transcendental Meditation. Biblical meditation can and should take place not only at a certain place at a certain time, but all throughout the day. And it is much more about filling our mind rather than emptying our mind. It is filling our mind with God's truth. It is pondering what He says and its implications for our lives.

Let's Understand the Words

There are two "families" of words from the Old Testament (originally written in Hebrew) which, at times, are translated into some form of our English word *meditation*. Using the numbering system of Strong's Concordance, group one is related to words 1897, 1899, 1900, 1901, and 1902. Group two is related to words 7878, 7879, and 7881. These two groups are surprisingly interchangeable.

Together these words appear about 70 times in the Old Testament. Over half of these occurrences are found in the Book of Psalms. Why would this be so? Because this book, more than any other, flows out of the meditations of the authors.

The basic meaning of these two groups of words is no surprise. They have to do with *pondering, considering, contemplating, reflecting, repeating,* etc. So this is the basic meaning of meditation: *to think slowly and deeply about a topic.*

Joshua was commanded by God *to think often, slowly, thoroughly, repeatedly, and deeply* about God's law. David said that because God's law was his delight, he would *ponder, reflect, contemplate, consider, chew on, soak in, have an inner dialogue about, and swallow* what it said.

Let's Slow it Down

You can't hurry meditation. It takes time. You can't meditate with a microwave. You meditate with a crock pot. You don't meditate at a drive through window of a fast food place. You meditate at a multi-course dinner at a fine eatery.

In one sense, you can't meditate while you are multitasking. But in another sense, you should multitask while you meditate. That is, it is right to take specific time to meditate. It is right to set other things aside and ponder this one, particular word, phrase, or thought. And it is also right to meditate while you are doing many other things. While you are driving, ironing, walking, even watching TV or reading a book, this one, particular word, phrase, or thought keeps running through your mind.

> *You can't meditate with a microwave. You meditate with a crock pot.*

But these same Hebrew words are also translated with many different English words. Here is where some interesting surprises show up. In various English translations of Scripture these words are translated with words like *speak, tell, utter, talk, whisper, pray, rumble, musing, imagine, plot, think, moan, commune,* and even *complain.*

Let's Complain About It

Do you find it curious that one of the translations of these words is *complain*? In our desire to understand and practice Biblical meditation, let's look more closely at this.

In one sense, this gives us great hope. Since we all know how to complain – don't be so pious! – we all know something about meditation! Here is the key. Meditation uses the same *process* as complaining, but with different *content.*

When we complain, we mull the situation or topic over and over in our minds. We have imaginary conversations with people who aren't there and can't hear us. We look at it from nearly every imaginable angle. Like a football coach, we run and re-run the video situation over in our mind, stopping it at key points to get a better view and analyze each frame. This becomes our default setting. Whenever we are not thinking about something else, our mind defaults back to this topic.

> *Meditation uses the same* process *as complaining, but with different* content.

We think about it *day and night*. Each time we view this footage we see more and more of its implications upon us.

Then, every chance we get, we talk about it, share it with others, etc.

In a similar way, meditation is making use of the same process. But instead of using content that was in some way offensive to us, let's "mark that as a block and delete it" and insert Biblical content in its place. So, instead of developing a complaint about something that happened to us, use the same *process* of mulling it over, but use completely different content. Insert some truth from God's Word. Have the imaginary conversation. Run and re-run the video. Analyze it. View it from every angle, consider its implications upon your life. Then talk about it with anyone who will listen. Rehearse it every chance you get. And then talk about it some more. Do this *day and night*. That's Biblical meditation.

Let's Chew on It

Some of these Hebrew words are also related to a cow chewing its cud: rumination. This is also a great picture of meditation. A cow has four stomachs. Let's say Bossy, our family cow, takes a nice big bite of alfalfa or hay or its favorite grain. She chews it until it becomes swallowable. Soon, she swallows it into stomach number one. The digestive process takes its course and soon Bossy... well, let's just say the contents of that bite finds its way back to Bossy's mouth. This process happens because there is more nourishment to be gotten out of that bite. More chewing, another swallow, and soon, another, ahhh... visit back to the mouth. This process is repeated until the former hay lands in all four stomachs. Biblical meditation is the same, bite, chew, swallow, repeat.

Let's Be Consistent

About twenty years ago, I developed a pain in my foot that was nearly crippling. A few days later it was gone. A few years later the same pain returned. This time the doctor gave me some powerful pain pills. The next time it returned I found out I had gout. My doctor prescribed some daily medication (I call it "gout out"). Because I never want to experience that level of pain again, I take that medication daily and I always keep it nearby. Meditation is like medication. One dose does not bring about a cure. But taken over time it prevents much pain. Because I want the benefit of that medication to work in my system, I follow the doctor's order and take that pill every day, even when I have no symptoms.

Meditation is not a quick fix for a bad situation. It is a long-term process of letting His Word have its way in us which produces more and more of His character in us. Taken regularly, it will not only prevent pain, it will also build us up in the faith.

Let's Let it Grow

The King James Version of the Bible uses the phrase *the engrafted word* in James 1:21. The New International Version uses the phrase *the word planted in you.* We have an apple tree that produces 5 different kinds of apples. How is that possible? By grafting branches from different kinds of apple trees into the trunk of the tree.

We graft a branch onto a tree because there is a certain kind of high quality fruit inherent in that branch and there is a separate trunk with a strong root system. More and better fruit is produced because of this grafting.

We graft a branch onto a tree by making a clean cut and smoothing out the end of the branch and scraping the bark from a corresponding portion of the trunk. Then we hold the branch against the trunk by using external help such as wires and poles. We place a rag around the joint and keep it wet. After a few weeks we can take the rags and wires off and the branch remains in place. The sap has flowed from the trunk to the branch and the two have been united.

We can graft Scripture into our lives in a similar way and for similar reasons. In this illustration we are the old trunk and Scripture is the branch with fresh life in it. There is a certain kind of fruit inherent in passages of Scripture we need in our lives, such as humility, love, wisdom, vision, or hope.

By intentionally holding that passage of Scripture against our souls, using the external means of our mind, keeping it wet with the Water of the Spirit, the truth of that passage of Scripture will become part of us. We will see our lives changed by God's Word.

A few verses after James refers to this grafting process, he concludes... *But whoever looks intently into the perfect law that gives freedom, and continues in it—not forgetting what they have heard, but doing it—they will be blessed in what they do.*[85]

The word James uses that is translated *look intently* here is worth noticing. It is only used five times in the entire New Testament. Three times it describes people looking into Jesus' empty tomb, once to describe how angels look at our salvation, and once used by James at how we can look into God's Word.

When John got to Jesus' tomb before Peter, he *bent over and looked in* the tomb.[86] A moment later, Peter did the same thing.[87] A few minutes later, Mary followed their lead.[88] These were not casual observers. They were looking very carefully in amazement. Peter also describes how angels wonder about our salvation. They *long to look into these things.*[89] This is the word James uses to describe how we can and should look into God's Word.

When we look intently, continuously into God's Word, – – which is the source of real freedom – *bending over* so we can see everything that is there, there is a spiritual transaction that takes place. Just like John, Peter, Mary, and even the angels, we are amazed at what we see! A grafting of His truth into our lives is taking place. As a result, we end up living consistently with that truth. And as we obey His Word our lives will be more and more blessed. We will

---

[85] James 1:25
[86] John 20:5
[87] Luke 24:12
[88] John 20:11
[89] 1 Peter 1:12

experience more of His Life and Power through Biblical meditation.

Let's Swallow it

Let me come back to and expand the illustration above about Bossy and her cud. This time, let's not talk about Bossy, let's talk about us. We need regular nourishment to grow and experience physical health. We receive that nourishment through the food we eat.

What is the process that makes that happen? It begins when we take a bite of food. But just biting into the food gives us no nourishment. Neither does chewing it. It gives us flavor and (hopefully) pleasure, but no nourishment.

There is one more thing we need to do before we receive any nourishment. We need to swallow it. And once we swallow it, we don't have to choose to do anything else. After we swallow the food, the digestive system God has placed in us takes over and that food starts becoming part of us. It becomes skin, hair, heart, blood, etc.

The same process is true in the spiritual realm. Can we "eat" spiritual truth? The fact is, we have biblical examples of this. Two prophets, Jeremiah[90] and Ezekiel,[91] ate scrolls that contained God's words. Ezekiel was told to and Jere-

---

[90] Jeremiah 15:16 When your words came, I ate them; they were my joy and my heart's delight, for I bear your name, LORD God Almighty.

[91] Ezekiel 3:1 And he said to me, "Son of man, eat what is before you, eat this scroll; then go and speak to the people of Israel." (See Ez 2:8-3:3)

miah did it because it was his delight. Then, in Revelation, John gets to enjoy the same diet.[92]

How can we do that? We begin by taking a "bite" of some truth. This may taste good, like a good sermon, or a good truth from a passage of Scripture. But we don't receive any nourishment simply from taste. We can chew it, ponder it, and consider it, but still no nourishment. Just as in the physical realm, for us to receive any spiritual nourishment from the food available to us, we must swallow it. This is the key step in Biblical meditation.

How do we "swallow" a spiritual truth? Very simply by *intentionally agreeing* with it. We swallow it by saying "yes" to it. This is the primary meaning of the word, "amen." Having pondered a specific truth, I say something like, "That is a truth I want in my life. Yes, Lord, let that be true in me. Amen... I not only agree with it, but I want it applied right here, right now." When we do this, we begin a process that could be called spiritual digestion.

> *Just as in the physical realm, for us to receive any spiritual nourishment from the food available to us, we must swallow it.*

When we intentionally agree with a spiritual truth, that truth begins to become part of who we are. It begins to affect and impact our thinking, our talking and our acting. It is on its way to

---

[92] Revelation 10:10 I took the little scroll from the angel's hand and ate it. It tasted as sweet as honey in my mouth, but when I had eaten it, my stomach turned sour.

our motives, our actions, our attitudes, as well as our thoughts and our words. It will affect our schedule, our wallet, our hobbies, our relationships and our jobs. This is not the only thing we need to do, but when we swallow a truth, it begins to become part of us.

Let's Talk About it

One more aspect of meditation deserves some specific attention here: the use of our mouths.

The words of our mouth matter. This is a clear theme in Psalms and Proverbs as well as other parts of Scripture. For example in Proverbs 8:6-8 the voice of Wisdom says, *Listen, for I have trustworthy things to say; I open my lips to speak what is right. [7] My mouth speaks what is true, for my lips detest wickedness. [8] All the words of my mouth are just; none of them is crooked or perverse.* And later Solomon says, *The tongue has the power of life and death, and those who love it will eat its fruit.*[93] At least 11 verses in Psalm 119 alone mention the importance of words.[94]

Part of meditating on God's Word is the use of our words. Meditation is more than thinking. It should result in us using our words to agree with God's words. Listen to what David requests of the Lord. *May the words of my mouth and the meditation of my heart be pleasing in Your*

---

[93] Proverbs 18:21
[94] See Psalm 119:13, 43, 57, 72, 88, 103, 108, 130, 131, 139, and 171

sight, O Lord, my Rock and my Redeemer.[95] The meditation of David's heart and the words of his mouth were connected.

This connection is seen in a few other key places. *The mouths of the righteous utter wisdom, and their tongues speak what is just.*[96] And *My mouth will speak words of wisdom; the meditation of my heart will give you understanding.*[97] In this second verse it is obvious that our words and our meditation are related. In the first verse above, this becomes apparent when we understand that the word translated *utter* is the same Hebrew word translated in other places as *meditation.* My mouth should utter what my heart is meditating upon. And you will remember that some of the other ways this word is translated include, *speak, tell, talk, utter,* and *whisper.*

The Apostle Paul picked up on something related to the mouth and the heart that Moses said in Deuteronomy. In fact, he writes a mini-commentary on it in Romans. Read what Moses wrote in Deuteronomy and then what Paul wrote about it in Romans. Read the two passages enough times so you understand them individually, then compare the two passages. Notice what Paul adds and notice what he emphasizes. I have put the two passages side by side on the following page.

---

[95] Psalm 19:14
[96] Psalm 37:30
[97] Psalm 49:3

Deuteronomy 30:12-14	Romans 10:6-10
12 It is not up in heaven, so that you have to ask, "Who will ascend into heaven to get it and proclaim it to us so we may obey it?" 13 Nor is it beyond the sea, so that you have to ask, "Who will cross the sea to get it and proclaim it to us so we may obey it?" 14 No, the word is very near you; it is in your mouth and in your heart so you may obey it.	*6 But the righteousness that is by faith says: "Do not say in your heart, 'Who will ascend into heaven?'" (that is, to bring Christ down) 7 "or 'Who will descend into the deep?'" (that is, to bring Christ up from the dead). 8 But what does it say? "The word is near you; it is in your mouth and in your heart," that is, the message concerning faith that we proclaim: 9 If you declare with your mouth, "Jesus is Lord," and believe in your heart that God raised him from the dead, you will be saved 10 For it is with your heart that you believe and are justified, and it is with your mouth that you profess your faith and are saved.*

Notice these key points from these two passages.

- The Deuteronomy passage is not primarily about faith, but the Romans passage is. (Romans 10:6, 7, 9, 10)

- This faith produces change in us. It is how our spirits are saved and how our souls continue to be saved. (See Galatians 3:3 and Colossians 2;6-7)
- What we believe in our heart and what we say with our mouth both play a role in this faith and salvation. (Romans 10:8, 9, 10) In fact, what we believe in our heart should be spoken with our mouth.
- There are things we are not supposed to say and things we are supposed to say. (Romans 10:6, 7, 9, 10)
- The word of God is supposed to be in both our mouth and our heart. (Deuteronomy 30:14 and Romans 10:8)

So, meditation is incomplete until it affects our speech. Saying what God says about ourselves and the situations around us is a key part of meditation. Meditation helps us understand what God says. It then helps it get written in our hearts. It then allows us to talk and act consistently with what He says.

So, meditation is incomplete until it affects our speech.

This is what moves meditation from a mental activity to a powerful tool of spiritual growth.

What does it mean to practice Biblical meditation?

- To engage in slow, deep, thorough, repeated thinking about a truth.
- To talk over, muse upon, commune with, dialogue with Scripture and its Author.
- To invite a Biblical truth into your life so it will conform your life to it.

- To use the process of continually complaining but change the content to align with Scripture.
- To bite, chew, swallow, repeat.
- To graft God's Word into our lives holding it up against our soul.
- To let God's Word determine the way we talk about ourselves, others and the situations we face.

So, now that we have a grasp of what meditation does and what it is, let's look at some people in Scripture who were meditators. But first, let's pray. "Father, continue to give me a greater understanding of how meditation works in a person's life as I look at some specific examples of those who meditate."

Chapter 5

The amount of time we spend with Jesus - meditating on His Word and His majesty, seeking His face - establishes our fruitfulness in the kingdom... An unschooled man who knows how to meditate upon the Lord has learned far more than the man with the highest education who does not know how to meditate.

~ Charles Stanley

Some Examples of Biblical Meditation

Do we have any examples in Scripture of people meditating? If this is such an important way to interact with Scripture, do we see people actually doing it in Scripture?

Great question. Let's look at four people – there are many others we could look at – who spent time meditating on what God said.

Jesus

We might as well go right to the top! Let's look at Jesus. First of all, please note that even though Jesus was the unique God/Man, when He was here on earth, He learned everything He knew. It is obvious that He learned how to talk, walk, read, etc. It is very reasonable to think that His earthly father taught Him carpentry skills. And Scripture specifically says that *Jesus grew in wisdom and stature, and in favor with God and man.*[98] But most significantly, He learned obedience.[99]

So, as remarkable as it may seem, Jesus also needed to learn the Scriptures. During His time on earth, there was a time when He did not know their content. And later there was a time when He knew it very well.

Specifically, there is evidence that during Jesus' time of temptation He was meditating on the book of Deuteronomy. The historical setting for this book is as the Israelite nation was poised to go into the Promised Land. The original generation had died in the wilderness and now Moses was reviewing their history and their previous interaction with God. This was Moses' last opportunity to prep them for their next steps with God. God's desire was that the nation would now move into the place where they would accomplish His mission for them. This took place just east of the Jordan River.[100]

During Jesus' time of temptation he was close to the same geographic area as the Children of Israel were when the book of Deuteronomy was delivered.[101] He was also poised to enter into the next steps God had for Him. So, both the location and the setting were similar. But the pri-

---

[98] Luke 2:52

[99] Hebrews 5:8 Son though he was, he learned obedience from what he suffered

[100] Deuteronomy 1:5 East of the Jordan in the territory of Moab, Moses began to expound this law...

[101] See Matthew 3:1 and 4:1

mary evidence that He was meditating on Deuteronomy during this time is the way Jesus responded when the evil one challenged Him.

All three times Jesus responded by quoting Scripture. Do you know what book He quoted from each time? It was the book of Deuteronomy! During His forty days of temptation, I believe Jesus was meditating on the book of Deuteronomy. Therefore, when He was tempted by the evil one, it was very natural for Him to use what He had been pondering as His primary weapons against him.

Mary

Jesus' mother was a ponderer. If we listed all the Biblical people who experienced amazing things, Mary would have to be near the top of the list. The announcement from Gabriel, the birth of Jesus, watching Him grow, assisting in His destiny, rejoicing and grieving during His ministry, experiencing the agony of the cross and the ecstasy of the resurrection. She took it all in.

Twice in Luke's story of Jesus' birth, he mentions specifically that Mary not only remembered the events, but *treasured and pondered them in her heart*.[102] She did not just experience these events, she continually referred back to them in her mind. She processed them, wondered about them, considered them, and remembered them. Tradition

---

[102] Luke 2:19 But Mary treasured up all these things and pondered them in her heart. [51] Then he went down to Nazareth with them and was obedient to them. But his mother treasured all these things in her heart.

says that Mary, some 50-60 years after these events took place, was a key source of information as Luke wrote his account of Jesus.

She did not just experience these events, she continually referred back to them in her mind. She processed them, wondered about them, considered them, and remembered them.

More evidence that she spent time meditating on Scripture is seen in her God-inspired declaration when Elizabeth greeted her.[103] Every verse of Mary's declaration has at least one Old Testament reference in it. Some have multiple references. She was so familiar with the Psalms and the Prophets that she naturally (and supernaturally) mixed these truths together with her current situation into a beautiful statement of praise.

The Other Mary

There are three passages that feature Mary and Martha. Each is very instructive. In John 11, their brother, Lazarus, had died. When he was sick, they called for Jesus, but He did not arrive until after Lazarus had already died and been buried. As Jesus was arriving, Martha came out to meet Him and said, *Lord, if You had been here, my brother would not have died.*[104] In response to this statement, Mar-

---

[103] See Luke 1:46-55
[104] John 11:21

tha received a good and accurate teaching from Jesus about the future resurrection. But her brother was still in his tomb.

Soon, Jesus asks Martha to have Mary come to Him.[105] When Mary arrives, she falls at Jesus' feet and says the exact same words as Martha.[106] In response to Mary's statement, Jesus is moved to the point of tears and raises their brother from the dead! This is powerful intercession! I want Jesus to respond to me the way He responded to Mary. Why the difference in response?

Six days later, recorded in John 12, Jesus is honored at a meal. Lazarus, Martha, and Mary are all there. Martha is serving while Mary was pouring perfume on Jesus' feet that was worth, in today's value, somewhere around $50,000![107] The room is filled with the sweet fragrance. Some protested, but Jesus defended Mary's actions, receiving it as an anointing for His soon-to-be burial.[108] This is extravagant worship!

One more story. This time from Luke 10. Some time prior to the two events mentioned above, Jesus and His 12 hungry disciples show up on Martha and Mary's doorstep. I am guessing they got there just before noon. Martha got

---

[105] John 11:28 After she had said this, she went back and called her sister Mary aside. "The Teacher is here," she said, "and is asking for you."

[106] John 11:32 When Mary reached the place where Jesus was and saw him, she fell at his feet and said, "Lord, if you had been here, my brother would not have died."

[107] John 12:3 – about one year's wages

[108] John 12:7 "Leave her alone," Jesus replied. "It was intended that she should save this perfume for the day of my burial."

distracted by all that needed to be done to feed them. "Oh my! I need more bagels! And what am I going to serve with them? And what will they want to drink?"

At one point she was even a bit miffed that her sister was not helping her.[109] Mary, however, was, again, sitting at Jesus' feet. She was "distracted" not by the situation, but by Jesus Himself and what He was saying. Did you catch that? She was sitting at Jesus feet taking in every word He was saying. This is effective meditation!

In each of these passages, Mary is at Jesus' feet. In each of them, she is honoring Jesus, listening to Him. And in each of them, Jesus responds very positively to Mary. From these three stories we can learn a key lesson: *powerful intercession* (the John 11 story) and *meaningful worship* (the John 12 story) flow from *effective meditation* (the Luke 10 story).

The Emmaus Road Disciples

On the day of Jesus' resurrection there were two disciples walking from Jerusalem to Emmaus. They were very concerned about Jesus' death and were not aware that He was alive. That was about to change. As they walked and talked, Jesus entered the conversation. As He talked, their

---

[109] Luke 10:40 But Martha was distracted by all the preparations that had to be made. She came to him and asked, "Lord, don't you care that my sister has left me to do the work by myself? Tell her to help me!" (See Luke 10:38-42)

discouraged hearts soon changed to burning hearts.[110] Jesus' words made the difference.

He began talking to them from the Scriptures. The point of His talking was to help them see that He was the object of those Old Testament passages.[111] They heard enough that they wanted more. So, when Jesus was ready to leave, *they urged Him strongly* to stay with them.[112] Look at what Jesus did next.

30When He was at the table with them, He took bread, gave thanks, broke it and began to give it to them. 31Then their eyes were opened and they recognized Him, and He disappeared from their sight.

> As He talked, their discouraged hearts soon changed to burning hearts.

Let's look at what the disciples did. They heard Jesus teach them and wanted more. So, they urged Him to stay with them. They also sat down with Him at the table. They received what He offered them. Then their eyes were opened and they saw who He really was!

---

[110] Luke 24:32 They asked each other, "Were not our hearts burning within us while he talked with us on the road and opened the Scriptures to us?"

[111] Luke 24:27 And beginning with Moses and all the Prophets, he explained to them what was said in all the Scriptures concerning himself.

[112] Luke 24:29 But they urged him strongly, "Stay with us, for it is nearly evening; the day is almost over." So he went in to stay with them.

And what did Jesus do? He responded to their invitation to stay longer with them, He sat down with them. He took bread, gave thanks, broke it, and gave it to them.

Do you see how this is an illustration of Biblical meditation? The disciples heard some of what Jesus had to say, invited Him to stay and tell them more. They sat with Him, listening to Him, and He did not disappoint! With thankfulness, Jesus gave them what they needed and as they received it, they recognized who was in their presence.

This is meditation. Inviting Jesus to come and teach us, listening to Him, receiving what He offers us and recognizing more of who He really is.

If these are examples of people who meditated, what should happen when we meditate? What is the desired outcome or goal of meditation? We will address that next. But first, let's pray. "Father, with these examples in mind, now help me to know and embrace the primary goal of meditation."

Chapter 6

*The end of study is information, and the end of medita-
tion is practice... Study is like a winter sun that shines, but
warms not: but meditation is like a blowing upon the fire...
Green wood is not kindled by a flash or spark, but by con-
stant blowing.*
~ *Thomas Manton*

The Goal of Biblical Meditation

So, what should happen when we meditate? What is
the goal, the desired outcome of it?

One way, among many, to describe the goal of our salvation is that we would be conformed to the image (or likeness) of Jesus.[113] To quote a well-loved professor of mine,
"God loves His Son so much that He purposed to fill all of
heaven with those just like Him."[114] And, as I stated earlier, one way the Father refers to His Son is as the Word of
God made Flesh.[115]

---

[113] Romans 8:29 For those God foreknew he also predestined to be
conformed to the image of his Son, that he might be the firstborn among
many brothers and sisters. (See also Galatians 4:19)

[114] John Mitchell (founder of Multnomah University) in his Spiritual
Life Class.

[115] John 1:14 The Word became flesh and made his dwelling among
us.

So, the Word of God (the Living and Written Word) is designed to be written not only in history and on paper but in our lives, on our hearts. Its purpose is to shape our lives so that we become more like Jesus. This is a primary goal of Biblical meditation.

God has always wanted what He says to us to land in our hearts.[116] He wants us to have ears to hear[117] and a mind transformed to His will,[118] but that is part of the process, not His desired destination. The destination has always been our hearts. He knows that when they are in our hearts, they will then get lived out in our lives.[119]

God has always wanted what He says to us to land in our hearts.

Immediately after God gives the Israelites the Ten Commandments, He said, *Oh, that their hearts would be inclined to fear me...*[120] and *These commandments that I give you today are to be upon your hearts.*[121] The wise

---

[116] Deuteronomy 11:18 Fix these words of mine in your hearts and minds; tie them as symbols on your hands and bind them on your foreheads. And Ezekiel 36:26 I will give you a new heart and put a new spirit in you; I will remove from you your heart of stone and give you a heart of flesh. (See also Jerimiah 24:7)

[117] Matthew 11:15 Whoever has ears, let them hear. (See 13 other cross references)

[118] Romans 12:2 Do not conform to the pattern of this world, but be transformed by the renewing of your mind. Then you will be able to test and approve what God's will is—his good, pleasing and perfect will.

[119] Deuteronomy 30:14 No, the word is very near you; it is in your mouth and in your heart so you may obey it. (See also Deuteronomy 32:44-47 – specifically "they are your life.")

writer of Proverbs encourages his son to *Let love and faithfulness never leave you; bind them around your neck, write them on the tablet of your heart.*[122]

Then, in establishing the New Covenant, He says, *I will put my law in their minds and write it on their hearts.*[123] As New Covenant believers we should see this as a normal process for us. And Paul, the primary writer of the New Testament, was able to say to the Corinthian believers that *You yourselves are our letter, written on our hearts, known and read by everybody. You show that you are a letter from Christ, the result of our ministry, written not with ink but with the Spirit of the living God, not on tablets of stone, but on tablets of human hearts.*[124]

How does God's Word get written on our hearts? Just as the Holy Spirit was the agent of bringing the Living Word and the Written Word into this world,[125] so also He is the agent to write His Word in our hearts and conform us to the Son. Jesus said that when He left He would send the Comforter (the Holy Spirit) to guide us into all truth.[126]

---

[120] Deuteronomy 5:29

[121] Deuteronomy 6:6

[122] Proverbs 3:3

[123] Jeremiah 31:33 and Hebrews 8:10

[124] 2 Corinthians 3:2-3

[125] Luke 1:35 The angel answered, "The Holy Spirit will come on you, and the power of the Most High will overshadow you. So the holy one to be born will be called[a] the Son of God." and 2 Peter 1:21 For prophecy never had its origin in the human will, but prophets, though human, spoke from God as they were carried along by the Holy Spirit.

[126] John 16:13 But when he, the Spirit of truth, comes, he will guide you into all the truth. He will not speak on his own; he will speak only what he hears, and he will tell you what is yet to come.

Biblical meditation is much more than a mere mental exercise. It is a spiritual process whereby the Spirit of God takes the Word of God and mingles it with my spirit. The end result is that eternal truths are written in the deepest part of my life and I am more like the Savior. Just as the Holy Spirit hovered over the first creation,[127] He also hovers over His new creation[128] to make us like Jesus.

What is the goal of this process? The goal of Biblical meditation is to cooperate with the Spirit of God to let the Word of God get written on the hearts of the people of God.

Here is my friend, Steve, and his story…

> *The end result is that eternal truths are written in the deepest part of my life and I am more like the Savior.*

"Joy unspeakable and full of glory!" That seemed to be my signature verse, my life - at least for the first two years of my walk and relationship with the Lord Jesus. Then the "bottom" fell out. Or maybe the wonderful wave of the Holy Spirit I was riding washed me up on the beach. For the next year I struggled to get back the wonderful euphoria of joy and blessing in the Holy Spirit through a life of legalism. "Surely, if I could make God happy by doing all the right things

---

[127] Genesis 1:2 Now the earth was formless and empty, darkness was over the surface of the deep, and the Spirit of God was hovering over the waters.

[128] 2 Corinthians 5:17 Therefore, if anyone is in Christ, the new creation has come: The old has gone, the new is here!

then He would return all the wonderful benefits of His Spirit in my life," I said to myself.

Instead of joy, all I seemed to get was great depression. An honest friend said to me at the time, "You look like a rainy day walking down the street." And I felt like I lived in a dark cloud with little motivation, no joy, and much self-condemnation. After about a year of struggling with depression I ran into Romans 10:8, the word (of faith) is near you, in your mouth and in your heart... I realized that my heart was not pumping words of faith and life but instead it was pumping words of doubt and death through my thinking and self-talk. Little by little I realized I needed a new heart and it was only through replacing the old lies in my heart with new truth from the Scriptures that my heart would be changed.

But equally important as believing something different in my heart was to also speak different words with my mouth. I found Scriptures that addressed and showed light on the difficulties I faced in my thinking: the way I saw myself as compared to how God saw me. I thought on these Scriptures and I also spoke them often. At first it seemed hypocritical to speak such wonderful truths when I still felt awful inside. But I believed the truth in Scripture was more powerful than the wrong thinking and lies in my own heart.

Sometimes, my meditation process became very vocal. I found myself shouting loudly to "convince" my listening heart that we are making a change—to line up with God's Word rather than my old heart

69

and way of thinking! In about six months of this meditation process - my heart went from "pumping death" and unbelief through the subtle self-talk that runs throughout the day - to pumping a new flow of life through a new kind of self-talk that was full of faith, hope, joy and thanksgiving from all God is and does and wants to be in my life!

Since the goal is to have God's Word written on our hearts, how do we engage in the process of meditation? What do we do? That's next. But first, let's pray. "Father, I invite You to write Your Word on my heart! Now, show me some of the specific things I can do to make that happen."

Chapter 7

Meditation is the activity of calling to mind, and thinking over, and dwelling on, and applying to oneself, the various things that one knows about the works and ways and purposes and promises of God...It is an activity of holy thought, consciously performed in the presence of God, under the eye of God, by the help of God, as a means of communion with God.
~ *J. I. Packer*

The Process of Biblical Meditation

So, what is the process of meditation? How do we do it? Are there any specific steps to take?

In addition to the things mentioned to this point – inviting Jesus into the process, sitting with Him, slowing down to consider the implications of what He says, anticipating receiving from Him, anticipating the Spirit of God writing His Word in our hearts, etc. – there are three essential steps I have found to be helpful handles as I meditate. Whether you meditate all at one time in a specific place in a more disciplined manner, or whether you meditate "on the go," these steps can help you glean well from Scripture. They should not be seen as rigid steps. In fact, I have found they work best when they are melded together, but it is helpful to take them in a certain order.

Ponder

The first part of Biblical meditation is to think slowly, thoroughly, and repeatedly about the text. Read it s-l-o-w-l-y. As Paul charged his young friend, Timothy, *Reflect on what I am saying, for the Lord will give you insight into all this.*[129] As we reflect, the Lord gives us insight.

Generally when we read a passage of Scripture we read it at the same rate we would read the newspaper or another book. There is a time to do that with Scripture, but you can't meditate at a rapid rate. Pondering also means I read it much more carefully than I otherwise would. I am not looking only for the big picture as I ponder, I am looking for the details that are not on the surface. I am looking for things that can only be found as I look over, under, around and through the words.

> *I am looking for things that can only be found as I look over, under, around, and through the words.*

Pondering requires that I read the words over and over. Read them over enough times until you see things you never saw before. Then keep reading them over and over. It is not uncommon for me to read a verse or a passage dozens of times as I ponder through it. Sometimes this is in one sitting, sometimes this is done over several

---

[129] 2 Timothy 2:7

days or even weeks. Don't worry about exhausting the truths of the passage. You won't.

Pondering involves considering each word and each phrase from several perspectives. When I was in high school, the cheerleaders would lead us in a yell that illustrates this. "WE like our team. We LIKE our team. We like OUR team. We like our TEAM." Meditation is giving each word and each phrase in a text time to tell you why it is important. It may involve studying certain words and how they are used in other places in Scripture. Use a concordance, some word study tools, cross references, other translations of the Bible, or just an English dictionary to help with this.

It also involves asking questions about these words and phrases. Questions like, "What are the key thoughts here? Why did the author use this particular word? What is the relationship between this word or phrase and the others around it? How is this word used in other places? What was the author trying to say here? How did the first readers understand this thought?

> *Meditation is giving each word and each phrase in a text time to tell you why it is important.*

What is God communicating here?" It involves reading a verse or a passage over and over again – sometimes for days. It involves thinking about the thoughts on several occasions.

Finally, it involves listening to His Spirit. Throughout the process of pondering, continue to listen to and for the Holy Spirit. Listen for His answers to your questions. Listen for His comments and His direction.

This is a process that is worthy to do at specific times. And it is a process that is worthy to do in the midst of other things you are doing. Memorizing the passage of Scripture allows you to ponder on the go.

Personalize

Scripture is not like any other book. Other books were not written directly to you. In one sense, Scripture is. Its purpose is not simply for you to receive information, but rather formation and transformation. We get to interact with it not simply to know the content, but to know the Author. It's not just that we read the Word, it's that it also reads us.

One way we can do this is to "climb into the text and let the text climb into you." Changing pronouns is a good way to do this. As you ponder through the verse(s), put your name into it. The first line from John 3:16 would be changed from "For God so loved the world..." to "For God love (insert your name)..." Continuing on in that verse, personalizing it would mean you would change "that whosoever believes in Him would have eternal life" to "that since I believe in Him I have eternal life."

Another way we can do this is to intentionally agree with the text. What I do is literally talk to the text and say things like, "Yes, that's what I want in my life. I want You to do that right here in me. Come and do that in me! I receive that truth right here, right now." Make the process very personal. Become friends with the verse. Invite it to do its work in you. Invite it over to your house so you can spend time together.

Part of personalization is to recognize that, in His infinite ability, when the Holy Spirit wrote these verses, He had you in mind. You can talk to Him and ask Him questions. You can anticipate He will answer you. Listen to Him. Ask Him to write this truth on your heart. Talk to Him about specific areas of your life where you think you need this truth. Put the truth on like you would put on your clothes. Be intentional. Do it on purpose.

Prayer

Prayer is the best final step of Biblical meditation. You have not interacted with Scripture best until you have meditated. And you have not meditated best until you have prayed.

To this point you have been interacting with the text, here you interact with the Author. To this point you have seen what you can and should pray about. Now you are praying about those topics. To this point you have sought to gain a deeper perspective on how the text and your life relate to each other. Now you are asking God to narrow that gap and bring your life into alignment with that text. You are asking Him to bring your life into conformity with

His life. You are asking Him to let His Word, and Jesus Himself as the Living Word, become incarnate in you too. You are asking Him to write His Word deep into your life.

You have not interacted with Scripture best until you have meditated. And you have not meditated best until you have prayed.

But prayer is not only about asking. Prayer is the communication portion of a deep love relationship with the Most Important Being in the universe. So, it can and should include thanking Him, praising Him, adoring Him, as well as yielding to Him. At this point it may be very appropriate for you to pray for others who may need this same truth in their lives. As we saw from the three stories of Mary shared earlier, powerful intercession (seen in John 11) and powerful worship (seen in John 12) flow best out of effective meditation (seen in Luke 10).

Here is my friend, Daryl, her meditation story…

One of the most personally impacting times of meditation on the Scriptures transpired over a forty day pilgrimage during the Lenten season. I had decided to narrow the focus during my morning prayer time to Jesus' final twenty-four hours - a slow motion, if you will, of His Passion. I was looking for His responses to each event as He made His way through the announcement of the New Covenant in His blood at the Last Supper to His final cry, Eloi, Eloi, lama sabachthani? I wanted fresh insight into the weight of the "exchange": the Priceless for the sinner.

The early morning hours afforded the quiet atmosphere I felt necessary to linger in the shadow of the Cross and listen for the Holy Spirit to reveal the deeper understanding I longed for. My approach began with a brief passage from one of the gospel accounts of Christ's Passion, such as Jesus' comment to His disciples in Mark 14:34, My soul is deeply grieved to the point of death. I asked the Spirit to help me imagine the setting, the sound of Jesus' voice, perhaps what the disciples were thinking as they heard Him speak. I tried to place myself there as a witness to what was taking place, and search my own heart in response. I wanted to experience Jesus, and awaken my soul to what He experienced for me.

Because I desired an unveiling of the intimacy expressed during those twenty-four hours I also read other portions of Scripture tied to the morning's passage, however not necessarily cross references. The narrative of Christ's suffering in Isaiah 53 is an example. In addition, I used a book in which the author described many of the scenarios Jesus would have faced, shedding much light on the culture and practices of Roman/Jewish culture of that day.

Together, these tools provided some very vivid mental pictures of the struggles Jesus met both physically and spiritually. Daily I wrote my responses to "being there with Jesus" in my journal; and would conclude with writing another prayer which usually came in the form of an expression of love and gratitude for what He had done.

Without fail, a profound sense of His Presence stood with me each day as I grieved over the depth of my guilt and shame, and the horror of those same sins pounding the nails deeper into His holy flesh. Honestly, I had anticipated this response and even welcomed it. However, God clearly exceeded my expectations with an astonishing perspective of the Son of Man in His humanity. Here was the very condescension of the Eternal God, dismissing all His privilege and right, to "tabernacle" with His sinful creation.

I was completely undone before the Sovereign One who held my eternal destiny. In the midst of my agony, I heard my own voice crying out "Crucify Him!" Daily, as I poured over the Biblical texts, I waited in silence until He dispatched heavenly assurance that the Son of God had willingly done all this at the bidding of the Father. His suffering had paid my ransom. The transformation that occurred during those days continues to this day as my approach to God's throne room takes me beside Calvary's horror. Leaving the filthy rags of my desperation on that hill with Jesus, I take His hand as He leads me into His Father's Presence where He again condescends to hear my voice crying out, "Holy, holy, holy, Lord God Almighty! Who was, and is, and is to come!"

Do you see the process of Biblical meditation in Daryl's story?

- Ponder – Think slowly, repeatedly, carefully, about the passage of Scripture.

- Personalize – Restate the truths so they apply directly to your life. "Climb into" them and let them "climb into" you.
- Prayer – Make it a conversation between you and the Author. As He talks to you, talk back to Him.

If your regular times with the Lord include these three things, great! If they don't, I encourage you to incorporate them into it. As I referenced earlier, meditation can and should be a regular part of all your interaction with Scripture. There may be other things you do during a regular "devotional" time with Him, but I encourage you to let His Word get written on your heart through meditation.

So what are we to meditate upon? Have we been told to meditate upon any specific objects? Let's look at four specific topics Scripture invites us to meditate upon. But first, let's pray. "Father, would You now let me use this process to meditate upon these specific topics mentioned in Your Word."

Chapter 8

It is not mere reading, but meditation -- "meditate day and night," as the Psalmist says -- which extracts the sweetness and the power out of Scripture.
~ *James Stalker*

The Objects of Biblical Meditation

What should we meditate upon? What are some things we should be pondering? What should be the objects of our meditation?

The obvious answer to this question is "God's Word." When meditation upon Scripture becomes part of our regular spiritual diet, we will *grow in the grace and the knowledge of our Lord and Savior, Jesus Christ.*[130] But what parts or topics of Scripture should we meditate upon? There are at least four topics Scripture itself invites us to be meditating upon.

See Chapter 10 for some suggested references to use when you meditate upon each of the following topics. Don't be satisfied with my starter list. I encourage you to use cross-references, a concordance, or other tools to develop a more complete, personal list.

---

[130] 2 Peter 3:18

The Person of God

Now this is eternal life: that they may know You, the only true God, and Jesus Christ, whom You have sent.[131]

God is the most wonderful, the most complex, the most amazing Being ever! He is worthy of our meditation. As the hymn-writer said, "Thou my best thought by day or by night..." Even in eternity we will never be able to say we fully know this stunning Triune God.

So during this lifetime, one of the most fulfilling things we as humans can accomplish is to know more of the Father, the Son, and the Holy Spirit.[132] Each is well worthy of our study and our meditation. No matter what Scripture we are meditating upon, there is something there about God we can ponder.

The Book of Psalms provides three other specific topics for our meditation: the ways (the works) of God, the wonders of God, and the love of God.

The Ways (the Works) of God

Show me your ways, O LORD, teach me your paths.[133] *He made His ways known to Moses, His deeds to the people of Israel.*[134] *I will meditate on all Your works and consider*

---

[131] John 17:3
[132] See Jeremiah 9:23-24, Romans 11:33-36
[133] Psalm 25:4
[134] Psalm 103:7

all Your mighty deeds.[135] *They will speak of the glorious splendor of Your majesty, and I will meditate on Your wonderful works.*[136]

There is obvious interplay between the ways of God and the works of God. The way people do things tells us about who they are. In fact, when certain people do certain things in a certain way other people refer to what they do as "their way" of doing things. God has a way of doing things. His ways are not our ways. It is right and healthy for us to consider His ways, how they differ from our ways, and ask Him to teach us not only about His ways, but to do things His way.

And when we see the work of someone's hands, examine the quality of what they do, or when we read what they have written, or hear what they sing, we get to know them more. The same is true of God. We get to know Him, His desires for us, the quality of His nature, by looking closely at what He has done.

Notice His ways and His works in Scripture and in your life. Notice His patterns. Why does He do certain things in certain ways? Ponder the way He has worked in history. As you do, you will come to know Him more and more.

The Wonders of God

Let me understand the teaching of Your precepts; then I will meditate on Your wonders.[137] *Remember the wonders*

---

[135] Psalm 77:12
[136] Psalm 145:5

He has done, the miracles, and the judgments He has pro-nounced.[138]

If there is a distinction between the ways of God, the works of God, and the wonders of God, I suggest the wonders of God focus more on His miraculous acts. These are things we could never do. The ways and works are more natural and His wonders are more supernatural. Nevertheless, all of what God does is worthy of our consideration.

There are four major *wonders* in Scripture: Creation, the Exodus, the Cross (including our salvation) and the Resurrection.

Creation – It is so amazing to meditate upon God's creation, His big *wonder*.[139] We are creative because we are made in His image, but we could never create like He created. He created all there is from nothing. His mighty, intricate creation shows us not only His *eternal power and divine nature*[140] but many other attributes like His creativity, His wisdom, His beauty, His vastness, His brilliance, etc. It reminds us that we do not own this planet, He does. It humbles us, encourages us, teaches us, and corrects us. Taking time to ponder, reconsider, notice and keep noticing, remembering that *He made us and not we ourselves*[141] keeps us on an even keel.

---

[137] Psalm 119:27

[138] Psalm 105:5

[139] Psalm 19:1 The heavens declare the glory of God; the skies proclaim the work of his hands.

[140] Romans 1:20

[141] Psalm 100:3 (note)

The Exodus – Over and over, Israel told their story and especially how God brought them out of Egypt.[142] This was the major *wonder* in their nation's history. The people knew the story well because they told it often. In fact, they were directed to remember it annually in the Passover meal. This was a *wonder* God did not want them to forget. This reminds us that we should regularly reflect on our own exodus from bondage to freedom.

The Cross – But the major *wonder* of God is seen at the cross of Jesus. It deserves our careful and ongoing meditation. I am convinced that everything we need to know about the relational nature of God is seen best as we look at the Cross and what Jesus accomplished there. Here we see His love, here we see His wisdom, His righteousness, His justice, His mercy, and His grace. Here we see both the ultimate example of the evil of sin and the goodness of God. Here we see servanthood. There is nothing else in history as significant as the cross of Jesus Christ! It is right that we think about it, sing about it, talk about it, and live differently because of it.

Years ago, I heard a friend of mine say during communion that "If it were not for the cross of Jesus, there would be no need for the Bible." At first I recoiled at this thought. But as I pondered it, I became convinced it is true. Were it not for the cross, what would God have to say to us? That is worth pondering.

----

[142] See, for example, Exodus 15:1-18, Nehemiah 9:9-15, Psalm 136 (which includes both creation and the Exodus), and Acts 7:1-38

I am convinced that every-thing we need to know about the relational nature of God is seen best as we look at the Cross and what Jesus accomplished there... It is right that we think about it, sing about it, talk about it, and live differently because of it.

The Resurrection – The resurrection of Jesus is as unique as His Cross. There has, literally, been nothing else like it in all of history. All other religious figures died and are still dead. Jesus is not. His resurrection demonstrates His deity,[143] declares The Father's acceptance of Jesus' sacrifice,[144] and sets Him apart from all others.

Finally, in addition to these Scriptural wonders, it is also very good to remember the miracles He has done in our lives and in the lives of those we know. I have seen people's bodies healed, minds restored, spirits saved, and souls restored. These have no other explanation than being a *wonder* of God.

Often times when God did a miracle for the nation of Israel, He told them to build a memorial so they, and the next generation, would not forget.[145] The reason for the physical

---

[143] Romans 1:4 and who through the Spirit of holiness was appointed the Son of God in power by his resurrection from the dead: Jesus Christ our Lord.

[144] Romans 4:25 He was delivered over to death for our sins and was raised to life for our justification.

[145] Joshua 4:7b These stones are to be a memorial to the people of Israel forever. (See Joshua 4:4-7)

memorials was so the pondering could continue to the next generation.

The Love of God

Within Your temple, O God, we will meditate upon Your unfailing love.[146]   *Whoever is wise, let him heed these things and consider the great love of the LORD.*[147]

Since the Great Commandment is that we would *Love the Lord your God with all your heart and with all your soul and with all your mind,*[148] we often focus on our love for God. But Scripture says that *we love because He first loved us.* [149] It is only as we know His love that we are able to love Him and love others around us. Meditating on God's love convinces us of His great love for us. This, in turn, allows us to love Him and others.

May you grow in His grace as you spend time meditating on these topics. But don't stop with these topics. In addition to these, there is no part of Scripture you should not meditate upon. You can meditate on specific selected verses, paragraphs, chapters, a section of a book, or an entire book of the Bible. Don't stop the other ways you interact with Scripture. Continue to listen to it, read it, study it, and memorize it. But incorporate meditation into all your interaction with it. Any part of the Bible worthy to be

---

[146] Psalm 48:9
[147] Psalm 107:43
[148] Matthew 22:37
[149] 1 John 4:19

heard, read, studied, or memorized is also worthy to be meditated upon.

These are amazing thing to be meditating upon! Now I want to invite you to look over my shoulder as I meditate a bit.   But first, let's pray. "Father, these things blow us away! Who you are, Your ways/works, Your wonders, and Your love. These capture us and thrill us! Now, as I observe this demonstration of meditation, help me to see things more clearly."

Chapter 9

As you read, pause frequently to meditate on the meaning of what you are reading. Absorb the Word into your system by dwelling on it, pondering it, going over it again and again in your mind, considering it from many different angles, until it becomes part of you.
~ *Nancy Leigh DeMoss*

A Demonstration of Biblical Meditation

There is more than one pathway to good meditation. As I have written, there are common elements, but they flow together differently from person to person and even from day to day. What follows is a demonstration of how I am meditating on Psalm 19:7-11 today. Since my mind works faster than my fingers, I have not written everything that has passed through my mind.

Three quick points before you continue. First, I do not normally write as I meditate, except for a key thought or two, or unless some key pieces of something I have been thinking about come together. If you normally journal, then journal as you meditate. Second, there is no preferred time frame as you meditate. What follows took me longer than I normally meditate at any one time. Finally, it is not necessary to meditate on this many verses. Sometimes you may want to meditate on just one word, or a phrase.

My hope is for you to get a virtual glimpse into the actual process of my meditation in real time. This should not be seen as the way I always meditate, but rather the way I am meditating this time. *I will use this font to represent the words of my meditation.*

Father, as I turn to Your Word today, please write it on my heart. Please move it from words on paper that were written years ago and make it alive in the deepest part of my life today. Like You say in Hebrews... "Today, if I hear Your voice, don't let my heart be hardened!"[150] Let me hear Your Words today. Let my heart be soft, pliable, and receptive. Great Shepherd, speak in ways I can hear and understand. Let my spirit be sensitive to Your Spirit. I trust You and look forward to what You have to say today.

Psalm 19:7-11

The law of the LORD is perfect, reviving the soul. The statutes of the LORD are trustworthy, making wise the simple. [8] The precepts of the LORD are right, giving joy to the heart. The commands of the LORD are radiant, giving light to the eyes. [9] The fear of the LORD is pure, enduring forever. The ordinances of the LORD are firm, and all of them are righteous. [10] They are more precious than gold, than much pure gold; they are

---

[150] Hebrews 4:7

sweeter than honey, than honey from the honeycomb.
¹¹ By them your servant is warned; in keeping them
there is great reward.

I am reading these verses over a few times. I am getting
familiar with what is here. I see the primary topic is God's
communication to us. I see six couplets in verses 7-9. Each
one (except 9a) contains a synonym for God's Word to us:
His law, His statutes, His precepts, His commands, and His
ordinances.[151] There are probably some nuanced differ-
ences between these words, but the primary thought, as it
also is in Psalm 119, is simply that God wants to and does
communicate with us!

There is also a very positive effect in the second half of
each of these couplets: Revival of my soul, wisdom to the
simple, joy to my heart, light to my eyes, endurance, righteousness. *These are desirable things! I want these.*
Yes, Lord, bring these things and plant them in my
spirit. Then in verses 10-11 I see the value of receiving
this God-communication. It is precious, more precious than
money or great food. Those who receive it are warned and
rewarded. *Father, make these things part of my life.*

---

[151] The fear of the Lord is mentioned in the fifth couplet. This re-
lates to God's communication to us in that as we spend time hearing
what God says, we will develop a healthy fear of the Lord. From my
previous studies on this topic – from verses like Psalm 111:10, 112:1,
Proverbs 1:7, 8:15, 9:10, etc. – my working definition of the fear of
God is "The knowledge of God that assures me that He loves me too
much to let me violate His principles of life with no consequence,"

I am reading this passage over several more times. I read it slowly. I am not in a hurry. I bounce back and forth between the verses. As I read it, I am inviting these truths to sink into my heart. I am intentionally agreeing with these truths.

Yes, Lord, Your law is perfect. It is just exactly what I need to have my soul be revived. Your statutes are trustworthy. I can and do trust what you say. There is wisdom there. As I absorb them, You do make me wise. You turn my simplicity into wisdom. Your precepts are right. They have and they do give me great joy. And Your commands certainly are radiant. They are brilliant! They do give my eyes light. I can see things differently, more the way You do, when I see them through Your Word. The fear of the Lord - which comes from hearing You through Your Word - is pure. When I see You and hear what You say, I do revere You. I do fear You. But I ask that you increase in me that reverential awe of who You are, how great You are, how terrible sin is, and how I can please You. And Your ordinances are sure. Everything You say is completely righteous.

What You say is more desirable to me than financial independence. I want what You say more than money. It is more desirable than the best dessert. It is better than all other temporal pleasures. You have warned me by them, and You have rewarded me for following them. Father, I am so thankful that You communicate with us! You are the best communica-

tor ever! The way You communicate and what You communicate is always just right.

Now, I am going through each line more intentionally. I will ponder, personalize and pray through each line.

The law of the LORD is perfect, reviving the soul. (v.7)

Your law - yes, the Ten Commandments, yes, Your Old and New Testament "laws" and commands, and also all the things You say. Not only Your specific commands, but everything You say is perfect. Whenever You open Your mouth, perfection comes out. What you say is exactly what my soul needs to receive life. You know my soul better than I do, better than anyone does. You know exactly what my soul needs to receive and walk in the life You have for me. So, Lord, as I hear and respond to Your perfect law today, revive my soul. Let Your life flow from Your Spirit to my spirit. Just as in the beginning You spoke and life came, so also today, speak and let Your life come to my soul.

The statutes of the LORD are trustworthy, making wise the simple. (v.7)

It is not just that Your communication is perfect, it is also trustworthy. Father increase my trust in what You say. I do trust You, but increase my trust. Let me trust You more today than I did yesterday. I have seen Your wisdom in Your Word many times. I am so grateful that I am more wise than I used to be. The wisdom of Your Word has been proved over and over in my life. If I had lived my life my way, it would be far less than doing it the way You have led me. Father, continue to show me my simplicity and Your wisdom. Let me reflect Your wisdom today in conversations I have with others. May more of Your wisdom be in this world today because I trust what You say.

The precepts of the LORD are right, giving joy to the heart. (v.8)

Your precepts, Lord, are simply right. Just like the right tool helps me do the job the right way, so also, what You say helps me do the right thing in the right way. And as I do, You release joy in my heart. Your joy is part of Your kingdom[152] one of the fruit of Your Spirit[153] and also the result of obeying Your "love" command.[154] Bring Your joy to me today. Let Your joy come through me to impact others today. As Your precepts come my way today, let me respond in such a way that I am both a joy receiver and a joy distributor!

The commands of the LORD are radiant, giving light to the eyes. (v.8)

And Your commands are radiant. They are brilliant. They are right. You tell us to do certain things or not do certain things because You love us and want the best for us. Because You know more about

---

[152] Romans 14:17 For the kingdom of God is not a matter of eating and drinking, but of righteousness, peace and joy in the Holy Spirit,

[153] Galatians 5:22 But the fruit of the Spirit is love, joy, peace, forbearance, kindness, goodness, faithfulness…

[154] John 15:10-11 [10] If you keep my commands, you will remain in my love, just as I have kept my Father's commands and remain in his love. [11] I have told you this so that my joy may be in you and that your joy may be complete.

how life works than I do, I humbly and joyfully bow before You and receive what You say. When Your words come, I am able to see things I otherwise would not be able to see. What You say sheds light on what everyone else (including me!) says. So, let me know what You have said in Scripture, let me hear what You are saying through creation (Psalm 19:1-2), let me hear what You are saying to Your church (Revelation 3:6, et. al.). And let me hear what You are saying to my heart throughout today, so that my eyes will be enlightened. Thank You for the light that comes in the midst of what is so often a dark world!

The fear of the LORD is pure, enduring forever. (v.9)

There is also a purity, and cleanness, to fearing You. I am so grateful for Your unending, trustworthy, comforting, love. And I am grateful that You are a God who is worthy to be feared. Thank You that You do not wink at my sin. When I look at Your Son on the cross, I know You do not take it lightly. What He suffered there causes me to tremble. Thank You that it a dreadful thing to fall into the hands of the living God (Hebrews 10:31). I want to stay as far away as possible from anything that contradicts what You say! You take my breath away with Your purity, Your vastness, Your power, and Your love. Let me never take sin lightly. Let me always remember that You are both a loving God and a holy God who, because of Your great love, cannot let me sin and get away with it. Thank You that there always has been and always will be great consequences to my sin. Father, as I fear You I am able to endure. I am able to stand. I am able to reject the wrong and embrace the right. The fear of the Lord is pure.

The ordinances of the LORD are sure and altogether righteous. (v.9)

When I look at Your ordinances, the rules You lay out for us to follow, I can find nothing wrong with any of them! They are altogether righteous. They are just right. They cover everything that needs to be covered and they leave nothing out. When You give us a command, when You tell us to do something, it always flows from Your righteousness and it creates more righteousness here on earth. When we follow Your ordinances, we have relationships that work. We have marriages working properly. We have children growing up healthy. We have schools that produce great students. We have communities that are safe. We have governments that function well. And we have congregations that are producing disciples of Jesus. Yes, Lord, Your ordinances produce "rightness." Produce more of Your "kingdom righteousness" in me and through me today. Let me know, embrace, and share Your ordinances with those around me.

They are more precious than gold, than much fine gold. (v.10)

I like gold. I think we all do. Money gives us the ability to do things. To build things and go places. To buy things and to bless other people. Gold is good. But there is something more valuable than gold. There is something more desirable than having financial independence. What You say is more valuable than money. It reminds me of Psalm 119:72. *The law from Your mouth is more precious to me than thousands of pieces of silver and gold.* Dollars are able to help us buy things, build things, and drive things. But Your Word - what You say to us - helps us buy the right things, build the right things, and drive to the right destinations. Lord, what You say gives life to us. Help me to be faithful with the "gold" you give me, but help me to always use it in a manner that lines up with what You say.

They are sweeter than honey, than honey from the honeycomb. (v.10)

And I like sweet dessert. I like the taste of a good meal. But what You say is far better than any good meal. The best food satisfies my mouth and my stomach for a few minutes or a few hours. What You say satisfies my deepest longings for years. It answers my deepest questions and it meets my deepest needs. I am grateful that I have never needed to choose between Your Word and Your provision. You have always been faithful to provide financially and physically. But I do pray that You would keep my mind and heart focused on the things that last the longest and mean the most.

By them is Your servant warned; in keeping them there is great reward. (v.11)

I am thankful for the privilege of being Your servant. I love saying "yes" to You. And I know that this servant has been warned on many occasions by what You have said. Your Spirit has used Your Word to warn me of the dangers of walking away from You. He has shown me Your love for me and the value of following Your ways instead of my ways. I have never regretted following You and Your ways. I can't say the same for following my ways. And You have rewarded me for following You!

My money and my time has gone farther when I use it for You then when I have used it for myself. You have rewarded me with favor from people and with the privilege of ministering to them. You have rewarded me by leading me to what I would clearly say are green pastures and beside quiet waters.[155] You have rewarded me with relationships with Marilyn (my wife), my kids, my grandkids, and many friends and family that are fulfilling. But clearly the greatest reward has been Your presence in my life. I can't put it into words, and I am grateful I don't have to! But Your presence in my life has been the best reward I could ever imagine. From that night on August 1st, 1968 when I first fully surrendered to You, till now, the best thing You have given me is the thrill of knowing You more and more.

So, Lord, please continue to speak. Give me ears to hear. Let Your Word be alive to me. Let me receive the life and the power of Your Word. May Your commands, Your precepts, Your ordinances, Your words to me continue to come and continue to shape me. Let them be as sweet as ever. Warn me. Reward me. Let me be like Jeremiah. (See Jeremiah 15:16) Let me

---

[155] Psalm 23:2

find Your words and eat them, and let them be a joy to my heart.

I hope this has been helpful to you. I want to emphasize a couple things before we move on. First, please only see this as one demonstration of meditation. You don't have to do it just as I have done it here. More importantly, listen to the Lord in the process. He will lead you to develop your own personal way of meditating.

Finally, let me give you some more suggested topics for meditation. But first, let's pray. "Father, as I take some steps in meditation, lead me. Let me use these suggestions to develop a strong habit of cooperating with You as You write Your Word deep into my heart."

Chapter 10

*The reason we come away so cold from reading the Word
is, because we do not warm ourselves at the fire of meditation.*
~ Thomas Watson

Some Suggestions for Biblical Meditation

As you implement the practice of meditation, here are
some suggested topics and Scriptures. There is much life
and power from God in Biblical meditation. I urge you to
receive it! I have received it and I deeply desire you to receive it as well.

Please do not overlook this section. Whether you use
my suggestions or find other topics to meditate upon is not
the most important thing. The most important thing is that
you meditate. All the other parts of this book point to this
chapter. *If you know these things, you will be blessed if you
do them.*[156] Knowing how to meditate will accomplish
nothing, unless you actually meditate. This book will only
be valuable to you as you do what is written in it. This is
where the "rubber meets the road." This is where you can
***Experience Life and Power of God through Biblical Medi-
tation***.

---

[156] John 13:17 (My emphasis)

In each of the sections below, the first Scripture is written out. After that I have listed a few other references. Many more references could be given for each topic. And of course, there are many more topics. I encourage you to dive into these and see how and what the Lord imparts to you.

Don't put yourself on a time-table. No need to hurry. Muse through these topics and references, see which ones may apply to you most, and meditate. You don't need to meditate on each of these topics or texts. Use them but don't let them be your master.

1 Person of God

1.1 Knowing God

Jeremiah 9:23-24

²³ This is what the LORD says: "Let not the wise boast of their wisdom or the strong boast of their strength or the rich boast of their riches, ²⁴ but let the one who boasts boast about this: that they have the understanding to know me, that I am the LORD, who exercises kindness, justice and righteousness on earth, for in these I delight," declares the LORD

Jeremiah 22:15-16   John 17:3

1.2 God the Father

Isaiah 40:10-11

¹⁰ See, the Sovereign LORD comes with power, and he rules with a mighty arm. See, his reward is with him, and his recompense accompanies him.

[11] *He tends his flock like a shepherd: He gathers the lambs in his arms and carries them close to his heart; he gently leads those that have young.*

Isaiah 40:1-31   2 Corinthians 1:2-4

Ephesians 1:3-6   1 Timothy 1:17

1.3 God the Son

Colossians 1:15-20

[15] *The Son is the image of the invisible God, the firstborn over all creation.* *[16]* *For in him all things were created: things in heaven and on earth, visible and invisible, whether thrones or powers or rulers or authorities; all things have been created through him and for him.* *[17]* *He is before all things, and in him all things hold together.* *[18]* *And he is the head of the body, the church; he is the beginning and the firstborn from among the dead, so that in everything he might have the supremacy.* *[19]* *For God was pleased to have all his fullness dwell in him,* *[20]* *and through him to reconcile to himself all things, whether things on earth or things in heaven, by making peace through his blood, shed on the cross.*

Luke 24:44   Philippians 2:5-11

John 1:1-2, 14   Hebrews 1:1-4

John 10:30   Hebrews 13:8

Ephesians 1:7-12   Revelation 1:8-18

103

1.4 God the Holy Spirit
   John 16:7-11
   ⁷ But very truly I tell you, it is for your good that I am going away. Unless I go away, the Advocate will not come to you; but if I go, I will send him to you. ⁸ When he comes, he will prove the world to be in the wrong about sin and righteousness and judgment:⁹ about sin, because people do not believe in me; ¹⁰ about righteousness, because I am going to the Father, where you can see me no longer; ¹¹ and about judgment, because the prince of this world now stands condemned.
   Romans 8:5-9   Ephesians 1:13-14
   Galatians 5:16-25   Ephesians 4:30

2   The Ways/Works of God
   Psalm 25:4-5
   ⁴ Show me your ways, LORD, teach me your paths. ⁵ Guide me in your truth and teach me, for you are God my Savior, and my hope is in you all day long.
   Exodus 33:13   Psalm 86:11
   Psalm 27:11   Psalm 103:7
   Psalm 51:13   Psalm 143:8

3   The Wonders of God
   3.1 Creation
      Romans 1:20

20 For since the creation of the world God's invisible qualities—his eternal power and divine nature—have been clearly seen, being understood from what has been made, so that people are without excuse.

Genesis 1 & 2   Job 38:1-7

Exodus 20:11   John 1:3-5

Psalm 19:1-6   Romans 8:20-21

3.2 Cross – Because the Cross is such a central topic in Scripture, I have opted to list out many more references than for the other topics. The story of Jesus and the Cross is the most amazing story of all time. I encourage you to soak these in. Receive the life and power of God that is resident in them.

Revelation 5:6-14

6 Then I saw a Lamb, looking as if it had been slain, standing at the center of the throne, encircled by the four living creatures and the elders. The Lamb had seven horns and seven eyes, which are the seven spirits of God sent out into all the earth. 7 He went and took the scroll from the right hand of him who sat on the throne. 8 And when he had taken it, the four living creatures and the twenty-four elders fell down before the Lamb. Each one had a harp and they were holding golden bowls full of incense, which are the prayers of God's people. 9 And they sang a new song, saying: "You are worthy to take the scroll and to open its seals, be-

cause you were slain, and with your blood you purchased for God persons from every tribe and language and people and nation.

10 You have made them to be a kingdom and priests to serve our God, and they will reign on the earth." 11 Then I looked and heard the voice of many angels, numbering thousands upon thousands, and ten thousand times ten thousand. They encircled the throne and the living creatures and the elders. 12 In a loud voice they were saying: "Worthy is the Lamb, who was slain, to receive power and wealth and wisdom and strength and honor and glory and praise!" 13 Then I heard every creature in heaven and on earth and under the earth and on the sea, and all that is in them, saying: "To him who sits on the throne and to the Lamb be praise and honor and glory and power, for ever and ever!" 14 The four living creatures said, "Amen," and the elders fell down and worshiped.

Genesis 3:15

Ps 22:1, 6-8, 14-18

Isaiah 52:13 –53:12

Zechariah 12:10

Matthew 27:27-56

Mark 14:12-26

Luke 9:28-36 (note v 31)

Luke 22:7-38

Luke 23:26-49

John 19:17-37

Acts 2:22-24

Acts 2:36 (note v 37)

Romans 6:5-7

1 Corinthians 1:7-25

2 Corinthians 5:15

Galatians 2:20

Galatians 3:1

Galatians 5:11

Galatians 6:11-14

Ephesians 2:11-18

Philippians 2:5-11

Philippians 3:7-18

Colossians 1:15-20

Colossians 2:13-15

Hebrews 9:16-21

Hebrews 12:1-3

1 Peter 2:24

3.4 The Resurrection

1 Corinthians 15:12-19

[12] But if it is preached that Christ has been raised from the dead, how can some of you say that there is no resurrection of the dead? [13] If there is no resurrection of the dead, then not even Christ has been raised. [14] And if Christ has not been raised, our preaching is useless and so is your faith. [15] More than that, we are then found to be false witnesses about God, for we have testified about God that he raised Christ from the dead. But he did not raise him if in fact the dead are not raised. [16] For if the dead are not raised, then Christ has not been raised either. [17] And if Christ has not been raised, your faith is futile; you are still in your sins. [18] Then those also who have fallen asleep in Christ are lost. [19] If only for this life we have hope in Christ, we are of all people most to be pitied.

Luke 24:1-53

Romans 1:4

Romans 4:25

Romans 6:4-14

Ephesians 1:19-23

Colossians 3:1-4

4. Love of God

Psalm 107:43

⁴³ Whoever is wise, let him heed these things and consider the great love of the LORD.

Romans 5:8

⁸ But God demonstrates his own love for us in this: While we were still sinners, Christ died for us.

1 John 4:10, 16a

¹⁰ This is love: not that we loved God, but that he loved us and sent his Son as an atoning sacrifice for our sins... ¹⁶ And so we know and rely on the love God has for us.

There are about 125 references to *Chessed* (the Hebrew word for God's love) in the Psalms. This word is translated into English with words like *(great) mercy, lovingkindness, unfailing love,* etc. None of them refer to the Psalmist's love for God. They are all refer to the Psalmist reveling in God's love for him. Here is a sample of those verses.

Psalm 5:7	Psalm 63:3
Psalm 13:4	Psalm 85:10
Psalm 36:5, 7	Psalm 86:5
Psalm 48:9	Psalm 89:1-2
Psalm 57:10	Psalm 90:14
Psalm 62:11-12	Psalm 92:1-2

Psalm 100:5 - This phrase (*The LORD is good and His love endures forever*) is used at key points in Old Testament history. Note the following verses in

their contexts. Based upon the results, it could be said these are the most powerful words ever sung.

1 Chronicles 16:7, 34	2 Chronicles 20:21
2 Chronicles 5:13-14	(note vv. 1-26)
2 Chronicles 7:1-3	Ezra 3:11 (note vv. 7-13)

Here are a few more verses about God's amazing love.

Exodus 15:13	John 3:16
Jeremiah 33:10-11	Ephesians 3:17-19
Psalm 107:1, 8,	1 John 3:1-3
15, 21, 31, 43	1 John 4:19
Psalm 143:8	

5. The Nature of the Word of God

Psalm 19:7-11

The law of the LORD is perfect, refreshing the soul. The statutes of the LORD are trustworthy, making wise the simple. ⁸ The precepts of the LORD are right, giving joy to the heart. The commands of the LORD are radiant, giving light to the eyes. ⁹ The fear of the LORD is pure, enduring forever. The decrees of the LORD are firm, and all of them are righteous. ¹⁰ They are more precious than gold, than much pure gold; they are sweeter than honey, than honey from the honeycomb. ¹¹ By them your servant is warned; in keeping them there is great reward.

Numbers 23:19	Matthew 5:17-19
All of Psalm 119	Luke 24:27, 31-32,
(section by section)	Luke 24:44-45

John 13:17

1 Thessalonians 2:13

2 Timothy 3:16-17

Hebrews 4:12

James 1:22-25

1 Peter 1:19-21

6. Our Salvation/Forgiveness in Christ

2 Corinthians 5:15

And he died for all, that those who live should no longer live for themselves but for him who died for them and was raised again.

John 1:12

John 3:16

John 20:31

Romans 10:9-10

Ephesians 2:8-9

Titus 3:4-5

1 John 1:9

1 John 5:11-12

7. Granting forgiveness to others

Matthew 6:14-15

14 For if you forgive other people when they sin against you, your heavenly Father will also forgive you. 15 But if you do not forgive others their sins, your Father will not forgive your sins.

Matthew 6:12

Matthew 18:21-35

Mark 11:25

Luke 6:37

Ephesians 4:32

Colossians 3:13

8. God's abundant grace

1 Corinthians 15:10

But by the grace of God I am what I am, and His grace was not without effect. No, I worked harder than all of them – yet not I but the grace of God that was with me.

John 1:14, 16-17   Romans 5:21
Romans 3:24   Titus 2:12
Romans 4:16   Hebrews 4:16

9. The role of good works in the life of the Believer
Ephesians 2:10

10 For we are God's handiwork, created in Christ Jesus to do good works, which God prepared in advance for us to do.

Isaiah 58:6-12   2 Timothy 3:17
Jeremiah 22:15-16   Titus 2:14
Matthew 5:14-16   Revelation 19:6

10. The image of God in us/The command to love others
Genesis 1:26-27

26 Then God said, "Let us make mankind in our image, in our likeness, so that they may rule over the fish in the sea and the birds in the sky, over the livestock and all the wild animals, and over all the creatures that move along the ground."

27 So God created mankind in his own image, in the image of God he created them; male and female he created them.

John 13:34-35

34 "A new command I give you: Love one another. As I have loved you, so you must love one another. 35 By this everyone will know that you are my disciples, if you love one another."

Genesis 2:7	1 Thessalonians 4:9-10
Genesis 9:6	James 3:9
Leviticus 19:18	1 Peter 1:22
Romans 12:10	1 John 2:9-11
Colossians 3:12-14	1 John 3:16-18

11. Our identification with Jesus

Romans 6:4

We were therefore buried with Him through baptism into death in order that, just as Christ was raised from the dead, through the glory of the Father, we too may live a new life.

Romans 6:5-10	Galatians 2:20
Colossians 2:20, 3:1	1 Peter 2:24

12. Overcoming temptation/sin

Romans 6:11-14

[11] In the same way, count yourselves dead to sin but alive to God in Christ Jesus.[12] Therefore do not let sin reign in your mortal body so that you obey its evil desires.[13] Do not offer any part of yourself to sin as an instrument of wickedness, but rather offer yourselves to God as those who have been brought from death to life; and offer every part of yourself to him as an instrument of righteousness. [14] For sin shall no longer be your master, because you are not under the law, but under grace.

1Corinthians 10:13   Colossians 3:1-14
2 Corinthians 5:15   Hebrews 12:1-4
Ephesians 4:17-24   1 Peter 4:1-4

13. Dealing with difficult situations/people

James 1:2-4

² Consider it pure joy, my brothers and sisters, whenever you face trials of many kinds, ³ because you know that the testing of your faith produces perseverance. ⁴ Let perseverance finish its work so that you may be mature and complete, not lacking anything.

Matthew 5:11-12   Ephesians 5:20
Mark 8:34-36   1 Thess 5:16-18
Romans8:28   1 Peter 2:19-21

How can you find other topics or Scriptures to meditate upon? Here are a few more suggestions.

- As you **hear** a Scripture referred to in a sermon or a song that catches the eyes of your heart, find where that passage is located and put it on your meditation list.

- As you to **read** Scripture, make a note of certain truths and ideas that stand out to you. These are ideas for meditation.

- As you **study** a passage of Scripture, incorporate meditation into your study.

- Consider verses you **memorized** some years ago. These would be good verses to go back to and think deeply and slowly about. And as you memorize new verses, do it for the purpose of meditation.

113

- Notice cross-references from familiar verses. These may turn into some of your favorite verses.
- Consider issues you are dealing with in your life. Use a concordance or other study tools to help you find verses related to these issues.

And Finally...

There is one more passage of Scripture I would like us to look at, and meditate upon. It is Luke's record of Jesus' well-known parable of the seed and the sower.

Luke 8:11-15

This is the meaning of the parable: The seed is the word of God. [12] Those along the path are the ones who hear, and then the devil comes and takes away the word from their hearts, so that they may not believe and be saved. [13] Those on the rocky ground are the ones who receive the word with joy when they hear it, but they have no root. They believe for a while, but in the time of testing they fall away. [14] The seed that fell among thorns stands for those who hear, but as they go on their way they are choked by life's worries, riches and pleasures, and they do not mature. [15] But the seed on good soil stands for those with a noble and good heart, who hear the word, retain it, and by persevering produce a crop.

The clear message of this story is that different people respond differently to spiritual truth. My hope and prayer is that you will respond like the fourth soil!

First of all, in verse 11, Jesus states that the *seed* He is referring to is the Word of God. When God speaks – in history and today – it has a "seed-like quality" to it. Just as we cannot count the number of apples contained in one apple seed, so we have no grasp of what one eternal word spoken by God can accomplish in our lives and in the lives of others we will touch. I encourage you to pay attention to all He says.

Next, please notice in verses 12 and 15 that Jesus is targeting our *hearts*. Understanding spiritual truth is important, but letting it impact our hearts – the deepest part of who we are – is essential to produce a crop.

Third, notice the four well-known types of soil. 1) Hard soil of the path which the evil one takes advantage of, 2) quick-to-respond soil that does not last because it has no root, 3) responsive soil that gets distracted by other "high priority" issues and chocked, and 4) good soil that hears, retains, perseveres and produces a great crop.

Fourth, notice that although we normally understand this as a passage related to initial salvation, it can also be applied to our ongoing growth. After we are in God's family, we are to grow in the same way we were born into it:[157] by believing what Jesus says. So, each time Jesus speaks to us, these same four options are before us.

You want your life to produce an abundant crop: not only enough for you, but enough for you to give away to others. So does Jesus. This takes place when His Word is written deep on your heart.

Meditation does this better than any other response. As you hear His Word, meditate upon it. As you read His Word, meditate upon it. As you study and memorize His Word, meditate upon it. As you do, you will not allow the

---

[157] Colossians 2:6 So then, just as you received Christ Jesus as Lord, continue to live your lives in him,

evil one take it away from you,(v. 12) you will not fall away, (v. 13) you will not be distracted by lesser things (v. 14) but instead you will retain it, keep at it, and it will produce an amazing crop. (v. 15) May you and others through you enjoy and be nourished by the harvest!

May you continue to **Experience Life and Power through Biblical Meditation**.

About the Books

"This is not a message I prepared just last week. This is something that has been part of my life for about 45 years."

Although it was not planned, this was a statement I made recently while preaching on the topic of Biblical meditation. No sooner had I said this then the crisp thought came, "Yes, and it is time you write on it."

Even though it had been a key part of my life for years, I had never thought about writing on this topic prior to that moment. So, over the next few weeks I pondered about how I was first introduced to this topic of Biblical meditation.

I was in High School when I was first encouraged to meditate on Scripture. A friend had recently attended a seminar. He did not normally teach my high school Sunday School class, but this week he shared with us some specific steps about meditating on Scripture he learned at that seminar. I was intrigued. It was about that time in my life I began to be serious about interacting with Scripture. Later I attended the same "Instituted in Basic Youth Conflicts" seminar and appreciated much of what I heard, including a few hours on the value and the practice of Biblical meditation. I know that Mr. Gothard also taught a variety of topics I wondered about, and that he has become a fairly controversial figure over the years, but I am grateful for what I learned from him on this topic.

A few years later I was at a very good Bible School studying God's Word with some very good teachers and students. I have no memory of anyone there teaching specifically on the topic of meditation, but this is where I began practicing it almost without knowing it. I spent a lot of time, in the classrooms, in my dorm room, while I was working, and while I was playing thinking about the Scriptures.

It wasn't until the late '70's, when I was pastoring a congregation, that I received more specific instruction on meditation. Campbell McAlpine, with whom I was privileged to have contact on several occasions, spoke at a retreat for our congregation. During this time he not only taught us but gave us time to practice this skill. I still have a very clear memory of some specific things God spoke to me during my times of meditation on that retreat. His book on the topic, *Alone With God*, has been very helpful to me.

As I pastored, my preaching style evolved from preaching what I had studied to preaching what I had meditated upon. This was a gradual transition I was not fully aware of until a few years into it. I continued to study, but my studying was not complete until I had meditated on the passage(s) from which I would be preaching. During this time I was regularly *Experiencing Life and Power through Biblical Meditation.*

This was about the same time I was challenged by the Lord to take Jesus' instructions on prayer – in the Lord's Prayer – far more seriously than I had ever taken them before. This combination (developing the process of meditating and a motivation to focus on the Lord's Prayer) became a major force and foundation for my entire life. I have written about this in *Living Prayer: the Lord's Prayer Alive in You*. In fact, this book is an expansion of the second chapter of that book.

I encourage you to find the Life and Power resident in the Lord's Prayer by meditating upon it. When Jesus told us to pray in that manner, I am convinced He meant it.

After 25 years of pastoring, the Lord reassigned me to become the director of International Renewal Ministries. This prayer ministry has allowed me to be with many groups of pastors in multiple-day prayer settings – Pastors' Prayer Summits. Here again I saw the Life and Power of God released through meditation and prayer. This time in a corporate setting. I have written about how you can help facilitate corporate prayer in *United and Ignited: Encountering God through Dynamic Corporate Prayer*. As you do, you can not only receive more of His Life and Power, you can pass it on to others.

Over the last decade or so Acts 6:4[158] has become a significant verse for me. These two foundational components of ministry (prayer and the ministry of the word) have helped to shape my life for years. Now I see the relationship of those truths to these three books. The first two deal with prayer: individual and corporate. This one deals with the most powerful way we can interact with His Word. It is

---

[158] Acts 6:4 ...and we will give our attention to prayer and the ministry of the word.

my great hope that you and others will grow in your relationship with Jesus and your ministry skills through them.

These books and many more related resources are available at www.lppress.net.

I express my heartfelt thanks to the following people for their input into this book. It is better because of your time and effort. Thanks to Jeremy Carmichael, Marilyn Fuqua, Dave Gadoury, Matt Hyde, Mark Matthews, Phil Miglioratti, Joshua Monen, Gary Parrett, Mark Pellitier, Jan Stahl, Dick Williams, Alvin VanderGriend, and Steve Zimmerman for reading an earlier manuscript and make suggestions. I appreciated all of them, even though I didn't use all of them. And thanks to Jeremy Carmichael, Scott Jones, Daryl Knudeson, Phil Miglioratti, and Steve Zimmerman for writing your stories of meditation and letting me use them here. They allowed people to see meditation "in real life."

About the Author

Dennis Fuqua (pronounced few-kway) has been the director of International Renewal Ministries since the year 2000 (www.prayersummit.net) and of Clark County Prayer Connect (www.ccprayerconnect.net) since 2012. Prior to that, he pastored for 25 years in Gig Harbor, Washington. In 1989, IRM, under the direction of Dr. Joe Aldrich, gave birth to the Pastors' Prayer Summit movement. Now Dennis helps shepherd this movement, which has spread to at least forty states and thirty nations. His love for the Written Word and the Living Word has lead him to engage in Biblical meditation as a lifestyle for many years.

He earned both his Bachelor's and Master's degrees in ministry at Multnomah University, Portland, Oregon.

He speaks often on the topics of individual and corporate prayer and meditation in congregations, conferences, classrooms, and retreats. His passion is to see the church relate best to God, itself, and to those who have not yet placed their faith in Jesus Christ. He is a member of America's National Prayer Committee and Mission America Coalition.

His articles have appeared in several magazines including *Pray! Magazine* and *Prayer Connect*.

He is also the author of the 2010 book ***Living Prayer: The Lord's Prayer Alive in You*** and the 2012 book ***United and Ignited: Encountering God through Dynamic Corporate Prayer***.

Dennis and his wife, Marilyn, have four adult children and seven grandchildren. They live in Vancouver, Washington.

Now It's Your Turn…

If this book has been helpful to you, if it has helped sharpen your ability and desire to experience more of God's Life and Power through His Word, if you see how it would help you and others know and love the Savior better, then there are some things you could do to encourage others to get it, read it, and use it.

- Talk about it with others, like your home or accountability group, or a Sunday School class. Encourage them to meditate on Scripture. Share your story with them. Perhaps start a group to encourage Biblical meditation.
- Share the book with others. As you read the book, did names come to your mind of people who should read it? If so, considering ordering copies for them and others as gifts. Quantity discounts are available.
- Or, encourage them to order one or more copies at the web site www.lppress.net.
- Share it with your pastor or other spiritual leaders.
- Mention it or post a brief review of it on your Facebook page or Twitter account or other social networks.
- Post a review on Amazon or other blogs or web sites. This is a great help. Or submit it to a magazine. We would love it if you sent us a copy of your review.
- If you would like to have Dennis come share on this topic with your congregation or group, he is an experienced and gifted communicator. Contact him by email at dennisfuqua@gmail.com.

Made in the USA
San Bernardino, CA
09 January 2015